PENGUIN BOOKS

Elderdesign

Rosemary Bakker holds a master of science with distinction from Hofstra University, and is a certified interior designer. She is a member of the American Society of Internal Designers, the American Society on Aging, the National Council on Aging, and Sigma Omega National Academy of Honors and Professional Society in Gerontology. She teaches workshops on Elderdesign to older adults, aging specialists, and design professionals throughout New York, including Parsons School of Design, the Brookdale Center on Aging, Hofstra University, the New School for Social Research, the United Federation of Teachers, the New York State Society on Aging, as well as various nonprofit foundations and HUD managers and service providers. Rosemary Bakker is also a consultant to corporations, the senior living industry, and private individuals. She is happily married and lives in Manhattan.

Elderdesign

DESIGNING AND FURNISHING A HOME

FOR YOUR LATER YEARS

Rosemary Bakker

ILLUSTRATIONS BY THOMAS KENNY

PENGUIN BOOKS

PENGUIN BOOKS
Published by the Penguin Group
Penguin Books USA Inc., 375 Hudson Street, New York, New York 10014, U.S.A.
Penguin Books Ltd, 27 Wrights Lane, London W8 5TZ, England
Penguin Books Australia Ltd, Ringwood, Victoria, Australia
Penguin Books Canada Ltd, 10 Alcorn Avenue, Toronto, Ontario, Canada M4V 3B2
Penguin Books (N.Z.) Ltd, 182–190 Wairau Road, Auckland 10, New Zealand

Penguin Books Ltd, Registered Offices: Harmondsworth, Middlesex, England

First published in Penguin Books 1997

1 3 5 7 9 10 8 6 4 2

Copyright © Rosemary Bakker, 1997
All rights reserved

Illustrations by Thomas Kenny

PUBLISHER'S NOTE
Every effort has been made to ensure that the information contained in this book is complete and accurate.
However, neither the publisher nor the author is engaged in rendering professional advice or services to
the individual reader. Accordingly, nothing in this book is intended as an express or implied warranty of the
suitability or fitness of any product, service, or design. The reader wishing to use a product, service, or design
discussed in this book should first consult a specialist or professional to ensure suitability and fitness for the
reader's particular liftstyle and environmental needs. Neither the author nor the publisher shall be liable or
responsible for any loss or damage allegedly arising from any information or suggestion in this book.

LIBRARY OF CONGRESS CATALOGING-IN-PUBLICATION DATA
Bakker, Rosemary.
Elderdesign : designing and furnishing a home for your later years
/ Rosemary Bakker.
p.   cm.
Includes index.
ISBN 0 14 02.5809 4 (pbk.)
1. Aged—Dwellings—United States.   2. Architecture—Human
factors—United States.   3. Interior decoration—United States.
I. Title.
NA7195.A4B34   1997
728'.084'6—dc21   96–48615

Printed in the United States of America
Set in Garamond No. 3
Designed by Judith Stagnitto Abbate

A NOTE TO THE READER

*T*HIS BOOK is designed to be used in several different ways. If you want specific information on smart-aging design for a specific room, you can go directly to the chapter on that individual room.

If you are interested in specific environmental remedies for a particular physical condition, refer to chapter 9, "Designing for Specific Physical Conditions."

I've suggested a number of innovative products for seniors that are ergonomically designed and well made. I think you'll find that they add comfort to your life and ease many difficult household chores. Some are referred to by brand name, especially where I felt the manufacturer offered a unique or high-quality product. Most products I have mentioned are listed in the Resource Guide at the back of the book. Also, I've supplied a range of prices to give you some idea of the cost for each product, but since prices in the stores are constantly revised, no price can be guaranteed.

ACKNOWLEDGMENTS

*T*HIS BOOK is dedicated to my courageous and loving mother, whose personal experience inspired me to write *Elderdesign*; to the memory of my father, whose love will always be a guiding force in my life; to my incredible sisters and brothers (thanks for sharing the journey); to Dr. Jeffrey Rosenfeld, for having confidence in me and opening many doors; to Wendy Wolf, my terrific editor at Penguin, whose insight and guidance made this book a reality; to Joan Snyder, for her friendship, lyrical writing style, and help with the book; to Jonathan, my jewel of a husband, for all his loving support and countless hours of patience while I labored away; and to all people everywhere, may you age gracefully and safely in the home of your choice.

CONTENTS

A Note to the Reader v

Acknowledgments vii

CHAPTER 1   Home Is Where the Heart Is 1

CHAPTER 2   Designing for a Lifetime 7

CHAPTER 3   Safety and Security in the Smart-Aging Home 23

CHAPTER 4   Living Rooms and Activity Centers 39

CHAPTER 5   Gardens and Outdoor Spaces 49

CHAPTER 6   The Smart-Aging Bedroom 65

CHAPTER 7   The Smart-Aging Kitchen 77

CHAPTER 8   The Smart-Aging Bathroom 99

CHAPTER 9   Designing for Specific Physical Conditions 113

CHAPTER 10 The Caring Community 149

CHAPTER 11 The Action Plan 163

Resource Guide 177

Bibliography 203

Organizations 209

Index 219

Elderdesign

CHAPTER 1

Home Is Where the Heart Is

EVERY DAY each of us grows a bit older and—with luck—wiser. The aging process is probably imperceptible, whereas the wisdom is obvious to everyone—or so we all choose to believe—but the process continues in any case, like it or not. As a nation, America has aged to the point where, for the first time in history, citizens over sixty-five outnumber those under twenty-five. This trend is not expected to reverse itself anytime soon. More than six thousand Americans are turning sixty-five every day, and the fastest-growing segment of the population is men and women over eighty-five; the growth of this group alone is expected to increase 42 percent by the year 2000.

The changes these new demographic realities will create will reverberate in society dramatically over the next several decades and on many different levels. From the choice of how we will spend our tax dollars to the selection of magazines we will see on the newsstand, seniors, by virtue of their majority status, will have a louder voice and constitute an ever wider constituency. New services, new products, indeed, whole new communities are springing up to accommodate the needs and desires of those who are moving into the second half of their lives. Generally, more relaxed workdays and less demanding family schedules provide seniors the opportunities to develop new interests in life. But it is also true that one of the most significant changes that accompanies advanced years is altered physical needs and abilities. In your home, what you need most is a safe environment that reflects and responds to your current physical needs. This need, however, does not automatically mean a new home! In fact, many elders are reluctant to leave the homes where their families were formed and their most cherished memories founded. But as often as not, many find their homes inadequately designed for less-active living. Seniors often find that although home is where the heart is, safety and comfort seem to lie elsewhere.

Don't assume that aging, deterioration, and disease go hand in hand. We haven't found the proverbial fountain of youth, but as a nation, we are aging more slowly and staying healthier than at any other time in history. The Center for Demographic Studies of Duke University informs us that while the percentage of elders in the nation has increased dramatically and life spans are lengthening, elders are also staying healthier, more vibrant, and active for much more of their lives than ever before.

Even though disease is not inevitable as you age, invariably some physical changes will occur. Science may soon find an explanation and, even better, a cure for the different conditions that often develop with age, but until that time, arthritis, less acute vision, and other impairments are common ailments for most people toward the end of a lifetime, however long that lifetime may be. Physical changes manifest themselves at different ages, depending on the individual, but some experience difficulties early in their fifties or sixties. Health limitations are scarcely a reason to cut back on any activities that give you enjoyment in life, but it *is* reason to create a living environment that can accommodate any existing limitations or those you anticipate later.

The Home Environment

Whether you're very young or very old or anywhere in between, you should look at your residence periodically to determine whether it suits you. If you're thinking that you would like to keep one permanent home for your entire life, there are design changes you should make to create the safest, most comfortable home for you at each stage of your occupancy. You probably went through a similar process if you had children—child-proofing a home if there was a toddler about, pulling things down. But the big difference now is that you're doing it for yourself or for a parent, who can (unlike a two-year-old) help you make decisions about adapting the environment. These same life span design features are even more important if you're thinking you're past the age where you want to move again and relish the thought of knowing you can age at home, regardless of any physical limitations you might later develop. In both cases and in a situation where you're just not certain where you will be living in the future, incorporating smart-aging design elements will attract a wider group of buyers if and when you want to sell your home.

And if you're already a senior who is thinking about where you wish to spend your retirement years, it is essential that you evaluate whether your current home will provide you the security, comfort, and independence you want to maintain. It is never easy to make clear-headed decisions in the midst of a health crisis. You may be lucky enough never to experience one, but it is wiser to evaluate the merits of your living environment when you are healthy and able to do so without any pressures or anxiety.

Public policy makers are increasingly aware that it's in society's best interest to provide elders with special assistive devices or home modifications that enable them to live capably in their own homes for the rest of their lives. The government's concern is primarily financial, because we now recognize that institutionalized care in a typical nursing home costs more than *forty thousand dollars a year*. But even more important, individual families are reaching the same conclusion for emotional, rather than financial, reasons. The simple fact is that most elders—87 percent according to the American Association of Retired Persons (AARP)—would prefer to live and die in their own homes and never have to depend on institutional care.

When older adults begin to worry about managing at home on their own if they become incapacitated, or when their children start to think about the safety of their aging parents without household help, it makes much more sense to analyze the problem rationally by examining the adequacies of the home rather than the physical capacities of its residents.

How often have we heard the story of a mother or a father who fell while bathing and broke a hip, then were in need of nursing home care; or seen a colleague lose productive time at work, worrying about a parent no longer able to negotiate stairs, trapped on the second floor all day?

These concerns would not be necessary if homes were properly designed for our entire life span. Instead, the newer ones often reflect the viewpoint of a youth-oriented culture, and the older ones reflect the design precepts of a bygone era. Many homes can be renovated, adapted, or retrofitted, however, with low-cost products or can be remodeled to incorporate elder-friendly features that add safety and security for older residents. Even the addition of kitchen gadgets that cost less than ten dollars can greatly ease daily tasks that may have become unmanageable for an individual with arthritis.

Personalizing the House

There are certain design principles that constitute the foundation in building a life-span home, whether you are starting from the ground up or renovating an existing home. These principles translate the primary objectives of safety and comfort into practical reality, and for this reason, they should be rigorously observed. But the most important element of any home design is the individuality it reflects. Your home should embody *your* needs, *your* preferences, and *even your* eccentricities.

First, you must learn to look at your house in a new light. Evaluate your living space with a systematic approach that includes an understanding of the elder generation's needs. Starting from outside the house, then working your way in, look at every room not only from the customary viewpoint of aesthetics, but also from an informed perspective of functionality—how you actually *use* the room, regardless of its "official" name or designation.

When you learn to see your home from the viewpoint of elderdesign, rather than how you've always used it, you'll begin to see what shortcomings there are for the way you want to live. For example:

- When your children were small and entertained themselves on rainy days with jungle gyms and a Ping-Pong table, you were thrilled to have a large enough garage to keep them amused; but would the toys find a better home at a charity now and would the space be more logically used for an at-home office, a hobby center, or even turned into an efficiency apartment if a caregiver is required?
- When your teenage daughters locked themselves in the bathroom for hours experimenting with new makeup, you were glad not to have a downstairs bathroom that enabled you to see Madonna look-alikes emerging; but would a downstairs bathroom now be more convenient, given the number of stairs that separate the two floors of your house?
- If you recall your husband's skiing accident that kept him in a wheelchair during recovery, you now might want to think about making your living space more accommodating for mobility aids such as walkers or even wheelchairs; his inability to get into the bathtub may have been funny when the entire family was around to help, but chances are a replay in his eighties would be less comical.
- Reading in bed with high-powered flashlights after lights-out may have been exhilarating for your kids, but you probably wouldn't embrace the necessity of continuing the tradition; elders require much

higher levels of lighting to see properly, and every room, hallway, and entry point of the house should reflect this reality.

As we age, our needs in our residential settings change. They sometimes become greater, depending on our health, and sometimes, even acute. If your family includes someone who is ill and especially if the diagnosis is a progressive disease, realism dictates that you evaluate the patient's long-term needs. Institutionalized care is *not* necessarily your only choice, and for many, home care in a properly designed setting is the most reasonable solution.

Caregiving can be a profoundly satisfying experience, but it should be made as easy as possible with design changes in the home to ease the needs of the patient as well as those of the caregiver.

My goal is to help you implement the following three basic steps required to create a home environment that is comfortable and safe for all age groups:

- You will learn to look at your home with the perspective of a geriatric specialist, noting features that, in light of current research, are likely to present problems to elders and identifying suitable solutions.
- You will be guided through each room of the house, even through outdoor spaces, and learn what products and construction ideas work best with physical limitations common among older adults and what features are well suited to specific health conditions.
- You will learn to focus on the importance of your own individual habits and lifestyle preferences that, when incorporated into a residential environment, define that home as yours and yours alone.

CHAPTER 2

Designing for a Lifetime

INTERIOR DESIGNING is the art of combining that which is both practical and pleasing; to be successful, a room can't just *look* good—it has to function and fit *your* living needs. The design must function properly and be pleasing *to you,* regardless of abstract standards of design, because it is *your* personal space! A design for a young, active family almost certainly would not work for an elderly couple; a design that would be functional and attractive for a group of young women sharing a household might be insufferable for a widower living alone. So while different homeowners—or even the same ones at different stages of their lives—may want to adapt the space to their current circumstances, it is still entirely possible to design for the present without ignoring the future.

Designing also contains an element of time. We all know of homes that look dated soon after being decorated, because they were so oriented to current fashion trends that when tastes changed, the design or "the look" didn't age gracefully. And what is true in design fashion is also true in design function. With endless time, money, and energy, updating is not a problem, but if any of these qualities is in short supply in your life, it is far wiser to design your home with the long term in mind and not be forced to redesign at every stage of your life unless you choose to.

Long term, of course, means different things to each of us, and few of us live lives today that are predictable even in the short term. But a home is an asset with a long-term life. Unlike other highly personalized items, such as clothing that we pass on to others or throw out when our tastes change, a home will be resold. The new owner's circumstances may be radically different from your own, but if your home has sufficient built-in flexibility to accommodate life-span differences, it will have much greater resale value.

Design Principles for a Smart-Aging Home

The key in designing for a lifetime is to observe good design principles, while acknowledging your own personal needs and preferences. Incorporating the basic construction and design elements in a house that would enable you or anyone else to live comfortably in the same structure for a lifetime is first a matter of attention to the following five principles:

1. The home must be "barrier-free" to accommodate mobility aids (walkers, canes, wheelchairs, etc.).
2. Physical support structures and environmental safety systems must be incorporated where there are hazards such as stairs, slippery floors, or low lighting.
3. Appropriate lighting must be installed, both indoors and outdoors.

4. The "minimal effort" test should be applied to anything that requires manual operation or physical exertion.

5. Color should be used both aesthetically and functionally.

BARRIER-FREE HOMES

Living longer does not mean losing your health, and it certainly does not mean losing your independence. But in the process of aging, there is a gradual sensory and physical decline that all of us will experience, to a greater or lesser degree. There is always the possibility, however remote, that at some point you may need a mobility aid. Designing to accommodate wheelchairs or walkers entails attention to many details; the most important ones are wide doorways and the turning radius in smaller rooms such as bathrooms. All doorways should be thirty-two to thirty-six inches wide, and every room should include a five-foot turning radius (that is, a cleared area five feet in diameter, in which to turn a wheelchair or walker). Doorsills also impede mobility aids and should be removed to create a smooth floor surface between rooms.

PHYSICAL SUPPORT
AND ENVIRONMENTAL SAFETY

Some degree of relative frailty is bound to accompany aging, particularly for an individual older than eighty. Researchers tell us that the most hazardous room in the home is the bathroom, and knowing this, it is easy to anticipate the problem of a potential fall. Grab bars should be installed not only in the bathroom, but also in any place in the house where relatively strenuous physical effort is required. Secure railings should be available for all staircases and transition areas such as hallways that must be traversed by anyone needing assistance.

Good design means safe design. We know that 80 percent of the deaths from falls in the home happen to older adults. The U.S. Public Health Service also informs us that in their estimation, two-thirds of all deaths related to falls are potentially preventable. After falls, the second most frequent danger for elders in the home is fire. Eliminating the known causes for both falls and fires in every area of the home greatly reduces the probability that either will occur.

LIGHTING

Less acute vision is usually part of the normal aging process. Not only is much brighter light required for proper vision, but the eyes are less able to adjust quickly from a light environment to a dark environment. Intense light must therefore be provided for task-specific areas as well as for transition areas such as hallways, where a change from natural outdoor light to dimmer, artificial light can be troublesome. You must pay attention to the quality of the light as well as to the quantity. Full-spectrum lighting is ideal. Known also as "chromalux lighting," it is available as regular bulbs or fluorescent tube lighting. Full-spectrum lighting closely resembles the spectral distribution of sunlight, providing the clearest color with a minimum of glare. Eliminate glare wherever possible, since those with reduced visual acuity find reflected glare particularly bothersome.

MINIMAL EFFORT TEST

Good design for a lifetime recognizes that arthritis and other prevalent joint conditions may reduce both fine and gross motor skills. With the advent of new industrial design for household appliances and other products, from doorbells to oven dials to sink faucets, you can compensate for decreased motor skills without sacrificing any aesthetic content. You can also incorporate the need for less bending, lifting, stretching, and kneeling merely by making height adjustments; thus storage units and other, often-used spaces become more accessible to the less acrobatic.

COLOR

We often think of color as merely an expression of taste, but, in fact, it can be used not only to design a beautiful room, but also to accommodate reduced vision. By using contrasting colors on the edges of furniture, the risers on stairs, or on the grab bars of the bathroom wall, you can add warmth and vivacity to a monochromatic color scheme. At the same time, the contrasts can make limited vision a much less troublesome problem in anyone's home by outlining and demarcating edges.

Design Personality for a Smart-Aging Home

Observing the design principles is important, but it is, after all, *your* home. It must reflect your personality, your needs, and your particularities. Manufacturers are responding to the growing needs of the mature market, producing smart-aging products and furnishings in an array of beautiful colors, shapes, and sizes. You can choose from a wide variety of attractive products that can help you age gracefully *and* in style, at home. The best approach toward redesigning your home is to follow this simple plan:

- Evaluate your current home.
- Evaluate your life and your needs.
- Evaluate your budget.

EVALUATING WHAT YOU HAVE

It's time for your home audit. Until you understand what you already have and what problems exist, you won't know where to begin to make your home appropriate for your life span. So let's begin with the exterior of your home, then work our way to the interior. The audit is a simple orientation of awareness to smart-aging design; ideally, you will eventually be able to answer *yes!* to every question or condition. But if not, don't worry about tackling the entire list in one afternoon. Especially if you're doing this to plan for future needs, you can think of it as a renovation process that takes place over many months or even years. So establish your priorities and get the project started. I'll be discussing each of these elements and concepts in more detail in the room-by-room chapters that follow this overview. You may have questions as a result of the walk through, so make note of them for later review.

OUTSIDE CHECKLIST   YES NO

1. Safe and easy entry/exit from main door to parking
area   ___ ___
2. Handrails on both sides of the stairs   ___ ___
3. Ramp or chairlift to front porch or to inside garage if
required   ___ ___
4. Loose paving stones or cracks in walkways or patio
are patched   ___ ___
5. Adequate lighting for security and safety   ___ ___
6. Easy-open latches on front and back doors   ___ ___

7. Stairs in good repair   ___ ___

8. Shelf near door to rest packages when entering   ___ ___

9. Retractable awnings to reduce interior heat gain in summer   ___ ___

10. Landscaping that blocks summer sun and allows winter light   ___ ___

11. Low-maintenance exterior materials such as aluminum siding   ___ ___

Notes: _____

_____

_____

BARRIER-FREE CHECKLIST   YES   NO

1. Unimpeded routes from room to room, and within rooms   ___ ___

2. Floor sills that could cause tripping or impede mobility aids have been removed   ___ ___

3. Area rugs have been securely taped   ___ ___

4. Doorways are all 32 inches wide or more   ___ ___

5. Doors and doorstops have been removed if they present barriers   ___ ___

6. Wheelchairs and walkers can be used where necessary   ___ ___

7. Furniture does not impede clear passageways for mobility aids   ___ ___

8. A downstairs bathroom with large, roll-in shower is easily accessible   ___ ___

9. The downstairs bathroom has a five-foot turning radius   ___ ___

10. Adjustable shelves in closets and cabinets for easy reach   ___ ___

Notes: _____

_____

_____

SUPPORT AND SAFETY CHECKLIST   YES   NO

1. Grab bars in bathtub or shower area, attached
securely to wall   ____ ____

2. Grab bars near toilet, attached securely   ____ ____

3. Railings on all interior staircases   ____ ____

4. Cooktop is electric or induction, with no open flame   ____ ____

5. Nonslip flooring in bathroom and kitchen   ____ ____

6. Antiscald valves in showerhead and bathtub spout   ____ ____

7. Telephone jack in bathroom and other often-used
rooms   ____ ____

8. Emergency communication system installed in home   ____ ____

9. Ample electrical power to prevent blown fuses and
power failures   ____ ____

10. Circuit breakers located accessibly on first floor   ____ ____

11. All fire alarms are hardwired and appropriately placed   ____ ____

12. Floor extension cords run across floor have been
replaced with additional outlets   ____ ____

13. Extension cords on countertops have built-in circuit
breakers   ____ ____

14. Exterior doors have easy-to-operate dead bolts   ____ ____

15. Automatic timer or shutoff valve on electric
appliances   ____ ____

16. Fire extinguishers are accessible and in working order   ____ ____

Notes: _____

_____

_____

LIGHTING CHECKLIST

	YES	NO
1. Bright light available for each specific activity area	___	___
2. Level lighting throughout home, including hallways	___	___
3. Night-lights in hallways, bathrooms, and bedrooms	___	___
4. Light switch or sensor light installed at entrance to every room	___	___
5. Three-way switches on all stair lighting	___	___
6. Outdoor lighting can be turned on and off from indoors	___	___
7. Waterproof light installed in shower area	___	___
8. Mylar or sheer curtains cover windows for glare reduction	___	___
9. Blinds or drapes cover windows where outdoor night-timelight is bothersome	___	___
10. Kitchen work areas are brightly lit	___	___

Notes: _____

_____

_____

MINIMAL EFFORT TEST

	YES	NO
1. Round door and faucet knobs are replaced with lever action	___	___
2. All light switches are converted to rocker switches	___	___
3. Crank adapter installed on windows	___	___
4. Motorized switches to open/close heavy window coverings	___	___
5. Kitchen and other storage cabinets are adjustable	___	___
6. Food preparation area includes easy-grip utensils	___	___
7. Kitchen has comfortable chair for sitting and height-adjusted work surface suited to sit-down	___	___

8. Controls on appliances are easy to read and operate ___ ___

9. Tension on windows is adjusted for easy opening ___ ___

10. Bathtub has hand support for easy entry/exit ___ ___

11. Lever faucets or lever adaptors over knob faucets ___ ___

Notes: _____

_____

_____

COLOR CONTRASTING TEST   YES NO

1. Upholstered furniture contrasts with background
walls and with floor ___ ___

2. Bedspread is color-contrasted with bedroom carpeting ___ ___

3. Grab bars in bathroom are color-contrasted with wall ___ ___

4. Towels in bath and kitchen are color-contrasted with
wall ___ ___

5. Kitchen work surfaces are light colored ___ ___

6. Wall switches have color-contrasted cover plates ___ ___

7. Appliances have colorful, large-lettered dials ___ ___

8. Edges of first and last step on all staircases are
highlighted ___ ___

9. Telephones have colorful, large-lettered, well-lit
numbers ___ ___

Notes: _____

_____

_____

EVALUATING YOUR LIFE AND
YOUR NEEDS

Designing a smart-aging house requires not only an assessment of your present home, but also an honest appraisal of your life situation. Designing a house in your twenties is different from designing one in your sixties. Similarly, anticipating the need to include a variety of environmental design features that address the general needs of most elders is a different task from designing for your own family members whose particular health conditions are well known. In thinking through the questions that follow, be honest and be careful. It will surely save you time, money, and aggravation once you begin the design process.

AGE: What is your current age and what is the likelihood that you will be in your house for the next decade or more? If you expect to be living there in your sixties or to be housing a family member who will age into their seventies and eighties, then take a serious inventory of the design changes that need to be made to accommodate normal aging conditions as well as the possibility of handicaps. National studies show that only 5 percent to 10 percent of adults in the sixty-five to seventy-five-year-old age group require assistance with daily activities, but more than 40 percent of those over eighty-five are in need of help for personal chores such as bathing.

PHYSICAL CONDITION: It may be that a health condition now makes living in your house difficult, regardless of age. This is not a reflection on your abilities or your physical capacities, but rather a question of poor design. A number of low-cost, high-impact changes could probably correct many of the inadequate design features immediately. For example, if you have trouble standing for long periods, consider all those changes that would let you work in the kitchen, bathroom, or any other area of the house while seated. It could change your outlook on life. Independence and the ability to take care of one's self at any age are key determinants in maintaining a healthy psychological frame of mind.

ANTICIPATION AND REALITY: You are the best and only person able to truly understand your needs; many family members and friends will have their own point of view and will offer their own advice, but listen to your heart. If you are a woman in your sixties whose husband is older, it is wise to anticipate the possibility of living alone, because the statistics show that 79 percent of all adults over sixty-five who live alone are women. If your objective is to remain in your home either on your own or with friends or another family member, plan now to make those modifications that will enable you to do so.

HOUSE PARTICIPANTS: Who else uses your house? Do you have a group of friends who frequently come over to cook together and to share a meal? Do other older or younger family members think of your house as a central gathering place for holidays and celebrations? If so, does the house really accommodate the needs of the young and the old who use it? Perhaps a few simple design changes would enable everyone to enjoy both the house and those special occasions that much more.

EVALUATING YOUR BUDGET

A limited budget for home modification does not prevent you from making many effective changes to your home; on the other hand, an unlimited budget doesn't guarantee a perfectly successful redesign. The key is to understand your own personal needs and to match them on a priority basis with your financial ability.

Chapter 11 includes information on financing techniques and borrowing options, but the only person able to establish the budget for the work is you.

If there are no individual health considerations in your case, and your objective is to incorporate smart-aging designs into as many aspects of your house as possible, you should begin with this information: The most common chronic conditions in the over-sixty-five age group are arthritis, heart disease, and vision loss. From a home design perspective, these conditions translate into a requirement for modifications that accomplish the following goals:

- Lessen dependence on appliances and other home design features that require fine motor skills;
- Eliminate the need for strenuous physical exertion where possible, especially the need to climb stairs;
- Improve lighting and color contrasting throughout the house.

For as little as one hundred dollars (or thereabout), you can improve your home lighting dramatically by buying five automatic night-lights: two for the stairs, one for the bathroom, one for the hallway, and one for the bedroom; in addition, you'll still have enough money left over to buy a standing lamp (a torchère) for the living room.

The following two theoretical budgets, one ten times larger than the other, accomplish the same goal. One clearly does so with a greater degree of luxury, but both have the desired impact of making the house suited to smart-aging. Prices for labor and materials vary, depending on where you live, and the same merchandise is often priced differently in different parts of the country. But the illustrations, nevertheless, indicate that smart-aging design is *not* entirely dependent on a big budget.

Two-Thousand-Dollar Smart-Aging Budget

IMPROVEMENT	APPROXIMATE PRICE
1. Wrought-iron railings on outside stairs	$350
2. Outdoor solar lighting near walkways	$200
3. Dead-bolt lock and lever door handle for front and back doors	$250
4. Transfer bench for bathtub	$150
5. Nonslip vinyl flooring in bathroom	$350
6. Colorful grab bars in shower and near toilet	$300
7. Handheld shower unit	$50
8. Bed rail to assist in getting out of bed	$150
9. Sensor light switches for lamps	$30
10. Handheld remote control units for appliances	$30
11. Ten-year lithium smoke detector	$20
12. Handheld "reachers" and pull-out wire shelving in cabinets	$100

Twenty-Thousand-Dollar Smart-Aging Budget

IMPROVEMENT	APPROXIMATE PRICE
1. Replacing exterior stairs with landscaped ramp	$3,000
2. Low-voltage lighting system on walkways and in garden	$350
3. Electronic video door-answering system with buzzer entry	$2,200
4. Replacing bathtub with walk-in shower	$6,000
5. Electric bed, adjustable in height and position	$1,800
6. Voice-activated home automation system lights and appliances	$4,200
7. Automatic fire-suppressant system in range hood	$700
8. Motorized units for height-adjustable kitchen cabinets	$1,750

As you can see, designing for a lifetime is not about spending money. It is about thinking through the most important changes that need to be made in your home to give you the maximum comfort and the highest degree of safety. The first step is to review your home security systems, those that not only prevent unwanted intrusion, but also facilitate quick assistance whenever it is required.

CHAPTER 3

Safety and Security in the Smart-Aging Home

*I*N THE broadest sense of the words, safety and security are what each of us craves most in life. To be emotionally, physically, and mentally at peace, we must take all necessary precautions to provide security in our homes. Accidents don't just happen; too often they are caused by negligence or carelessness in correcting an obvious problem around the house.

For elders, a sense of total security in one's own home is essential. Protection from physical hazards as well as from intruders can be largely assured by identifying potential problem areas in advance. The result will be considerable peace of mind not only for those who are aging but for those who are caring for them.

Protecting the Home Exterior

DOORS: There are many varieties of doors; those made of solid, heavy wood are the most secure, though they can be expensive. A metal door is equally secure and is highly recommended for ultimate safety. Far from looking like industrial castoffs, metal doors today often have foam insulation and weather stripping. And they can be treated with a wood grain finish to simulate the look of expensive carpentry. A peephole to verify the identity of the caller is available in most high-quality metal doors. A wooden door with a nonbreakable glass (or plastic) panel is an alternative if you want additional daylight in the entry hall. If your current door has a breakable glass panel, install metal grating over the panel on the inside or replace the glass with a nonbreakable acrylic panel. Not only does the door have to be solid, but also the door frame must be equally sturdy, because a good door on a weak frame will not deter burglars. The frame should be made of metal or hardwood, and it needs to be bolted into solid blocking behind the frame with long screws. All exterior doors should measure thirty-six inches to provide for easy wheelchair access if needed in the future.

Crime Prevention

1. The crime prevention unit of your local police department can offer additional assistance in making your home burglarproof. Some departments even offer free home security surveys.
2. Another valuable resource is AARP, which offers two helpful brochures on home security: *How to Protect Your Home*, #D395, and *How to Conduct a Security Survey*, #D396.

Safety features of the front entrance include handrails on the stairs and light fixtures illuminating the walkway, landscape, and porch.

If the house presently has sliding doors, you can secure them against forced entry by placing a wood block or metal tube in the floor track and by drilling screws through the stationary panel and into the door frame.

Remove screen doors during the months when you're not using them; dealing with one door at a time is often as much as anyone carrying packages can manage. In fact, if you mount a shelf at roughly the height of your waist, just outside the front door, it will provide a handy ledge when you're trying to juggle groceries and to unlock the door at the same time.

LOCKS: When purchasing new locks for your home and garage doors, buy the best you can afford. Low-priced locks are made from low-quality materials that can be easily forced open. It is not enough to have secure hardened steel or brass dead bolts on all exterior doors, although this measure is essential. The locks must also be easily managed by those with a limited range of fine motor skills. An ideal lock is one that releases a dead bolt at the activation of a single lever. Just as important as the lock is the door strike. Use a heavy-duty door strike, and attach it to a strong door frame with three-inch to five-inch long screws.

Another option for easily managed, secure locks is an electronic system, with a key, card, or touch-control locking system. An electronic touch-control system offers the added advantage of a remote control feature that, when combined with video intercom, allows an occupant to buzz in guests without going to the door. To integrate these two systems, you will need an electric strike plate, which can be difficult to locate. One source is Hanchett Entry Systems. The company manufactures a model that can be used with a dead-bolt lock. (For more information on video systems, see page 30.)

WINDOWS: Every window should have a secure lock to prevent unlawful entries. Window locks are available from your local hardware store for just about every type of window. Alternatively, for double-hung windows, drill an angled hole through the top frame of the lower window partially into the frame of the upper window. Then insert a nail or pin. Make a second set of holes with windows partially open so you can have ventilation without inviting intruders. For casement windows, drill a small hole through the latch frame and handle when the latch is in a closed position. Insert a nail through the hole to lock the window. For additional security, install decorative iron grills on the outside windows.

Ideally, every room in the house should have at least one window that can be opened by someone whose upper-body strength or manual dexterity is limited. This may mean retrofitting or replacing some windows that are hard to open. In an older house, it is also important to replace any rotted wooden windows because they present both a security risk and exposure to drafts.

Casement windows are relatively easy to open with a crank or lever mechanism, though these are ill-suited to the installation of portable air conditioners. On the other hand double-hung windows, which open from top to bottom, require more strength to operate but can be adjusted by loosening the screws on the tension rod inside the window frame.

Instead of replacing existing windows that are still serviceable, you can retrofit both double-hung and sliding windows with a crank and latch attachment, available from A-Solution, Inc. This mechanism allows the window to be opened with relative ease; for anyone in a wheelchair or with limited upper-body strength, this solution is ideal as long as the window can be reached from the chair.

DOORBELLS: Because you should keep doors locked from the inside at all times, it is essential to have a doorbell that can be heard from anywhere in the house. This doesn't have to mean turning up the volume! You can also install several chimes around the house, upstairs and down. For the hearing impaired, flashing lights that blink when the bell is rung can also be installed in one or more rooms. If you have only a modest hearing loss, a wireless chime doorbell can be installed. The transmitter is placed at the front door and the chime attached to the kitchen, den, or bedroom wall.

OUTDOOR LIGHTING: If the approach and entryways to a house are dark and forbidding, installing security devices such as locks may not be sufficient for maximum safety. Bringing lighting to the outside is relatively easy and can be comparatively inexpensive.

First, make certain the front door is properly lit, ideally with lights on both sides of the door or under the awning. Low-wattage frosted bulbs reduce glare and should be used with fixtures that cover the bulb from exposure to the elements. You might want to consider inserting "photo-cell" units in the sockets. These units automatically turn on at dusk and then turn off at daylight. A battery device can also be installed to provide intense, direct light over the keyhole. Key rings or key holders with a miniature flashlight attached are also available.

The pathway leading to the door should also be well lit with either solar path lights or low-voltage ground lights. Solar lights don't require any wiring and are therefore simple to install, but a climate with continual cloud cover or little sun will limit their effectiveness. A local home-center supplier will best advise you on the suitability of solar lights in your particular location. Low-voltage (12-volt) lights use far less electricity than conventional 120-volt systems and can be placed on a timer to switch on in the evenings. You can install infrared lights around the grounds or garage. Activated by motion, these devices automatically switch on when any moving object crosses the path of the beam; all too often, however, the unannounced visitor turns out to be a squirrel or a cat.

GARAGE: An electronic garage door opener that turns on bright light when the door is opened is an enjoyable luxury for all drivers, but it's essential for many elders. Take care to ensure that the entire garage door area is properly lit, not just the footpath that leads to the front and back doors.

Communicating with the World

Staying in touch with one's friends and family makes an important difference to elders who may begin to feel isolated by their diminished ability to pursue activities outside the home. Fortunately, a whole range of products makes communications relatively simple. Nor is social conversation the only important aspect of communication. Many daily needs, such as grocery shopping or laundry pick up and delivery, can be handled by telephone, extending a sense of self-sufficiency to the many who are unable to run multiple errands each day. Moreover, emergencies can and do happen to everyone; a communications system that facilitates speedy assistance offers critical peace of mind for elders who are at home and for those who are concerned about their welfare.

EXTERNAL COMMUNICATIONS
SYSTEMS

TELEPHONES: The necessity of running from room to room to answer a call, increasing the potential for a fall, is a problem resolved simply by adding more telephones. An adapter can be purchased that plugs into an electrical outlet, avoiding the necessity of any rewiring. Portable phones are another option, though they often lack the features that are most important to elders, namely, large numbers, volume adjustment (for both ringing and incoming voice volume), and an emergency, one-touch dialing button. In addition, many portable phones are not hearing-aid compatible. Phones already owned or leased can sometimes be adapted to provide a low-vision, large-numeral push-button option. Be certain, too, that the numbers you call most often can be programmed in for easy, one-touch memory dialing.

EMERGENCY RESPONSE SYSTEMS: There are several devices on the market that are useful in being able to call for immediate help. These emergency response mechanisms are small radio transmitters, enclosed in a pendant that is worn around your neck or wrist, much like a necklace or a bracelet. The emergency "alarm" is activated when you simply push a button. Most emergency response systems are designed to signal a monitoring center with twenty-four-hour staff. These units come with a small, two-way remote box that is usually placed in the home. When the user pushes the emergency button, the monitoring center is contacted. The staff will first try to reach the calling party through the two-way radio. If the user does not respond, the staff automatically calls for emergency assistance. An alternative emergency response system is one that does not signal a monitoring center; instead, when the button on the unit is pushed, a signal is sent to a console unit that is hooked up to your own phone. A prerecorded message (e.g., "This is Mary McIntyre, please send help") is played to a series of (usually five) telephone numbers you have selected. These units are less expensive than emergency response systems that involve an intermediary at a monitoring center, but there is a risk that no one will be reached at any of the numbers that are automatically dialed. For more information on emergency response systems, call or write to AARP, for its product report, Personal Emergency Response System, free booklet 12905.

INTERNAL COMMUNICATIONS SYSTEMS

Several types of internal intercom systems are available. Many of them are wireless and readily found at home improvement stores or department stores. An inexpensive wireless intercom makes communication easy for elders and leaves the caregiver freer to move around the house without the worry of being needed and out of hearing distance.

Another type of internal communications system is a picture intercom, often found in apartment building entrance hallways. The same type of unit is available for private home installation and allows you to immediately see the caller at your front door. By pushing the remote button located on the video intercom, you release a special electrical strike latch wired to the front door. This device is particularly helpful for anyone who is bedridden or who has trouble moving around, and it can often be installed in only three hours.

Environmental Controls

The level of environmental comfort one feels at home depends on whether its control system allows simple, quick adjustments of both temperature and light. The more elaborate control systems provide touch or even voice controls for separate zones. The system can be wired not only to change room temperature and lighting, but also to activate other appliances. Some systems turn off all interior lights and simultaneously turn on exterior lights while arming the security system. But without spending a fortune on elaborate electronic systems, it is still possible to allow occupants to control heat and light in frequently used rooms even if the occupants have physical difficulty in operating manual systems.

TEMPERATURE: Our requirements for warmer room temperatures customarily increase with age, and for the sick or frail, a room temperature maintained at 68 to 72 degrees Fahrenheit is generally too cold. For this reason, separate heating zones in a house are a comfort for elders, especially when a house is shared by others who prefer cooler settings. To avoid the cost of retrofitting an in-place heating system, space heaters can be used. To prevent tripping hazards, do not run extension cords to electrical outlets, especially if house occupants have low vision. For small-size rooms, you can buy space heaters that plug directly into the wall outlet itself. This is a safe and simple remedy as long as there are no flammable objects within three feet of the heater.

A second alternative is a radiant heat panel that can be attached to the ceiling by an electrician. Thermostatically controlled, this unobtrusive one-inch thick appliance heats within four minutes and can be turned on or off by an auxiliary bedside switch.

LIGHTING: In the normal process of aging, most adults experience minor changes in their vision that can be troublesome if compensating changes are not made within the living environment. Older adults not only require more light to see properly (three to five times as much as a twenty-year-old, in fact), but also lose the visual ability to adjust instantly to changing levels of light—for example, when entering a dark hallway on a bright sunny day. Consequently, attention should be paid not only to the overall quantity of light in the house and to the quality of specific task lighting, but also to transition areas such as an entry hallway, where a dramatic change from outdoor bright light to a dimly lit interior might cause accidents.

The light can be increased with higher wattage or with three-way bulbs. Most existing lamps can be converted to three-way lighting by buying a "touch-turn-on" adapter. Halogen bulbs offer bright light, especially for reading or sewing, but for people with light sensitivity, halogen bulbs may be too bright or glaring unless the bulb is shielded; some halogen lamps are made with a special filter. Halogen bulbs also produce excessive heat, so they are not recommended for use in hot climates. A 150-watt incandescent light provides gentle, warm tones, whereas chromalux bulbs (also called full-spectrum lighting) filter out the yellow rays that can dull visual perception. Fluorescent lighting has the advantage of being relatively inexpensive both to purchase and to operate. Its only disadvantage is that the light takes a few moments to come on to maximum output; and for specific work projects, supplemental direct light is usually required.

Safety Tips for Halogen Floor Lamps (Torchères)

Halogen torchères can be a fire hazard if not used properly. The bulb heats to a very high temperature, and the top of the lamp is an open-bowl shape, increasing the risk of fire if flammable materials drop in.

- Replace any 500-watt bulb with a cooler 300-watt bulb.
- Do not place a lamp near curtains or drapes; wind can blow fabric into the top of the bowl.
- Do not place the lamp in a high-traffic area where it might be knocked over by a pet or grandchild.
- Never touch a halogen bulb with bare fingers; the oils from the skin can damage it.
- Never drape clothing over the lamp.
- Turn off the lamp when you leave the room.

To avoid having to walk through a dark room, install illuminated light switches in the entryway of each room or hallway. Automatic night-lights in the bedroom, bathroom, and hallway are another precautionary measure, as are dimmer switches to lower light levels during the night.

SENSOR LIGHTING: A sensor switch can be purchased for approximately forty dollars and installed without new wiring. The device detects movement and turns on the lights automatically as you enter a room, but it can be deactivated by a switch. Just remember to turn the activator off at night if you don't want the lights to come on every time you roll over in bed. Wireless wall-mounted sensor lights are also available, with light output equal to a bright flashlight; they are ideal for use in small, dark spaces, including foyers.

While insufficient light is the most common problem in retrofitting a house for elders, too much light, especially glaring light, can be equally disturbing. Blinds or sheer curtains should cover windows that emit strong sunlight, and opaque lamp shades should cover any bare bulbs. Mylar covering on windows may also be adequate to reduce glare; this product offers the valuable advantage of insulation, screening out 50 percent of the summer sun and reflecting back 60 percent of the escaping heat during the winter. Reflected light on glossy surfaces such as highly polished wood furniture can be eliminated by using a fabric tablecloth, or on wood floors, by refinishing with a dull surface. Where high-gloss paint is too intense, as very high-gloss white often can be, an overcoat of matte finish will eliminate the glare.

ELECTRICAL SYSTEMS: Many older homes have outdated wiring and may require upgrading, especially in the kitchen if you are accustomed to using many different electrical appliances. If you find that your fuses often blow when you are using more than one appliance, ask an electrician to evaluate the adequacy of the overall wiring. If you find that rewiring is needed, ask about having your fuse box or circuit breakers installed in an area of the home that is well lit and accessible rather than mounted in the usual dark corner of the basement.

Wireless wall switch and remote control box.

If all that's required, however, are a few more outlets, you can generally accomplish this task with surface-mounted wiring along the baseboard or at a higher level (approximately eighteen to thirty inches from the floor), where it will be much easier to reach. Extra wall switches for a lamp can also be added without incurring the expense of an electrician by purchasing a unit that glues onto the wall; the lamp is then plugged into a remote control box, which itself is plugged into an existing electrical outlet. With this arrangement you don't have to cross a dark room to reach a lamp. Simple extension cords are always an option, but only those with built-in circuit breakers should be used to ensure maximum protection against fire. And tape or tack them down securely, so you don't trip crossing your brightly lit room!

GAS HEATING SYSTEMS: Gas heating systems generally offer clean, comparatively inexpensive heat, but they can, if turned on without proper ignition, cause invisible carbon monoxide to build up in the house. The gas system should be checked periodically by a licensed plumbing contractor for ventilation problems, faulty connections, or defective parts. The chimney and flue should be cleaned yearly. A carbon monoxide detector, installed near the gas heater, is always a wise precautionary measure especially if space heaters are being used.

SMOKE ALARMS: Building codes vary, but in general the fire department recommends installing a smoke detector in the hallway next to a bedroom. Additional units are required on each floor in a large home and should also be placed directly outside the kitchen, where fires so often begin. (New models are triggered by such minuscule amounts of smoke that placement directly within the kitchen is unwise; anything being sautéed will often bring the fire engines.) Batteries need to be changed twice a year; try to do it on a regular, easily remembered schedule, such as New Year's Day and the Fourth of July. Because smoke detectors are usually mounted too high to be conveniently reached, you may prefer to have an electrician hardwire the alarms, eliminating any worry about battery replacement. Ten-year lithium smoke alarms (although expensive) are another alternative if you want to be free of constant worry about changing batteries.

Mobility

If you spend a good deal of time at home, it is vitally important to be able to enjoy all of the house, not just one or two rooms. But where mobility of the occupant is restricted, it is crucial that the home be designed to anticipate and avoid problems and potential accidents.

STAIRS: Stairs are the number one consumer hazard and the cause of far too many falls by elders. New stairs should be built with treads that are eleven inches wide and seven inches high; these are general construction standards. But if you use a walker or have mobility problems, a four-inch height is preferable to the typical seven-inch riser. Similarly, a larger tread of eighteen to thirty-four inches may be more suitable than the standard eleven inches. Open risers are particularly dangerous, so to protect against the possibility of tripping, they should be closed off with a properly sized board nailed against the opening.

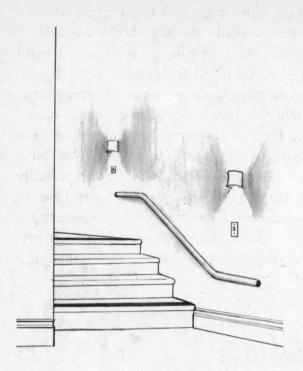

Features of smart-aging stair design include railing, lighting, and color outlining on edge of treads.

Retrofitting an existing staircase is generally more trouble than building a new one, but if an old staircase exists that is adequate except for one high step at the bottom, it may be possible to add an interim tread. Equally important are the addition of 1½-inch round handrails on both sides of the stairs. The rails should be securely anchored into wall studs to support the user's full weight, extend twelve inches, measure thirty-three to thirty-six inches from the height of the stair, and be 1½ inches away from the wall. Broken or uneven treads should be repaired right away, and any torn tread materials replaced.

Lighting is critical. It should be plentiful and bright at both the top and bottom step. Hallway lights should illuminate the entire stairwell adequately. Three-way switches at both the top and bottom of the staircase are also essential to allow you to turn the light on or off at either location, but if you do not want to install new wiring, there is a new wireless, three-way switch now available. You replace the existing wall switch with the base switch, and the wireless remote switch up to fifty feet away.

Tightly woven carpeting is the best covering for stairs; vinyl treads are another alternative, and some even come with color highlighting on the edge. This feature allows a person with low vision to see the edge of each stair more clearly; if the stairs are bare wood, applying glow-in-the-dark red tape on the edge of each tread will accomplish the same purpose. Painting the first and last step with highlighter is also a handy visual aid.

HOME ELEVATORS: Home elevators may become a necessity if an occupant cannot live comfortably on one floor of the house. There are essentially two options to consider: a device that rides on rails mounted to a load-bearing wall or a hydraulically powered unit. The first is the least expensive and requires no shaft but may present a noise problem for those who are particularly sensitive. American Stair-Glide Corp., manufacturer of the Minivator, likens the noise of their product to that of a small sewing machine. A backup battery pack may also be required for this type of system if there's a power failure.

Hydraulically powered systems are much more expensive but offer a variety of options such as automatic lighting, silent operation, room for two passengers (a patient and caregiver), and an emergency battery lowering system to prevent entrapment between floors during a power outage. If you're thinking about an elevator system, visit showrooms where units are being operated to evaluate the individual features, space requirements, noise level, and comfort of the ride.

DOORS AND DOORWAYS: Ideally, door openings should have thirty-two inches of clear space to accommodate a wheelchair. This width is not only aesthetically pleasing, with a feeling of elegance and grace, but also practical when moving through the space with packages or walkers. Door openings are not easily enlarged in older homes, though it's possible to simulate this change simply by removing the door itself, along with the doorstops. Also, be sure to remove the threshold barrier on the floor between the two rooms. Pocket doors are a useful solution in new construction or for narrow spaces such as closets and bathrooms. Purchase only high-quality doors with ball-bearing wheels that won't jump off the tracks and require very little effort to move.

FLOORING: For those who walk slowly or with difficulty, moving from one flooring surface to another can be hazardous. It's best to use one flooring material for all rooms throughout the house, other than for bathrooms and kitchen. The safest floor covering is dense low-pile carpet that absorbs sound, reduces heat loss, and cushions the severity of a possible fall. Wool or nylon composition is preferable for resiliency and flame resistance. Sheet flooring, either vinyl or linoleum, is another wise choice because it's easily cleaned and softer underfoot than ceramic tile. You will want to find the least slippery floor possible, and this quality is ordinarily measured by the "coefficient of friction," or COF. A high COF, one of 0.6 or higher, is generally a safe, slip-resistant floor. (If ceramic tiles are already installed in your house, they should be treated with a coat of nonslip paint.) Wooden floors with area rugs generally have a high accident rate, and not only among elders. Wood floors should have a matte finish, and if area rugs must be used, they should be securely fastened to the floor with two-way tape.

CHAPTER 4

Living Rooms and Activity Centers

M OST OF us are willing to put up with flimsy futons as college students, messy diaper pails as young parents, and blaring stereos as older ones, but empty nesters and elders are all too ready for the perfect living space—one that is not only attractive, but also easy to live in and to care for. If these qualities describe *your* desires, smart-aging design can help you achieve them.

When designing an interior living space, your primary considerations should be not only the choice of furnishings, but also how the space is to be used for leisure or "living" activities. Many historic houses and antique-show display rooms are magnificent to look at but would be sheer agony to live in. Appearance is

Key elements of an elder-friendly living room are ample illumination, supportive seating, and an uncluttered four-foot pathway through the room.

important because good taste and beauty make even the coldest days and the saddest moments of our lives more bearable. But a room designed only for looks is a room in which little living can actually be done; the lighting may be too dim, the fabric patterns too assertive, and the seating space too fragile for real comfort. Decorating a room is different from designing a room. The first is about beauty, whereas the second embraces aesthetics from the larger perspective of function and practicality. Remember, too, that how you use the room should dictate its design. It is not important that you have a formal living room and dining room if, in reality, 90 percent of your meals are enjoyed in front of the TV in the den. Your own reality should be the only determinant of your own design, and lifestyle magazines that tell you how to use your home should be read for entertainment, then donated to the library and ignored.

CHOOSING FURNITURE: It is no longer necessary to choose between pleasure and functionality or between an attractive look and an inviting seat. Designers today are as careful about how comfortable a chair feels as they are about how good it looks. Poorly designed chairs do not allow the proper alignment of the spine; they rotate the hips and cause discomfort. Select chairs with firm seats and solid supporting arms to provide assistance in rising. The chairs should not be too low or too deep, since both features make rising more difficult. If you have limited leg strength, add an "automatic rising device" that can assist you from a sitting to a standing position.

Reclining chairs reduce stress on the lower back for some users, but the mechanism for moving from an upright to a reclining position, or vice versa, must be one that is relatively easy to use. Choose one with either a mechanical lever on the side of the chair or automatically raises the user to standing position. Chairs that rock or glide are also comfortable, but an ordinary rocking chair is usually not a good choice because it tends to tip over easily.

Select colors for walls, fabrics, and floors from warm tones within any color group; a strong color accent can be added as a complement. A yellow sofa against a pale cream wall, for example, is both aesthetically restful and charming. Fabric selection should draw from small-scale pattern groups, with textured surfaces featured over slippery ones.

If you or someone you live with is a smoker, be certain that only one chair is used for smoking and that the chair is covered in flame-retarding material such as wool, wool blends, or heavyweight synthetics.

It's also important to think about how to arrange furniture, still mindful of how you use the room. Is it for entertaining? An older adult may be limited in hearing or sight, so the seating should be arranged at right angles, or on direct parallels, but not too far apart. If you like a traditional look, place the sofa against a wall with tables at both ends; each should have a table lamp with a three-way bulb. Is it for reading? Check the availability of good light. Can you see the best view from the chair you are most likely to occupy during the daytime?

The coffee table is generally in front of the sofa, with side chairs flanking it. The customary coffee-table height is twelve to fourteen inches, but a higher table, one that is roughly twenty-four to thirty inches, reduces the possibility of tripping over the table and lessens the amount of bending. Depending on the placement of the TV, a higher table may interfere with viewing, but if not, a medium-height coffee table will be more comfortable for eating or enjoying a cup of tea.

The notion of comfort, of course, embraces issues other than furniture selection, and, in fact, for some, comfort means being surrounded by personal memorabilia and various belongings with special significance. What's comfortable to one, however, may be merely clutter to another who uses the room. Be aware that, cumulatively, too many small distractions can make an environment too confusing for anyone trying to cope with mental or physical difficulties.

Other points to remember about furniture placement and living-room arrangements are:

- Scatter rugs or area rugs should be securely taped to the floor or removed.
- Carpeting with strong patterns or strong color contrasts within the pattern may be visually confusing and lead to misjudgments of spatial distances.
- Don't run electrical cords across the floor area where seating is available; it will always be a tripping hazard. Ideally, electrical cords should never be run across any expanse of floor, whether or not there is a seating group arranged in the area. Table lamps and other electrical items should be placed only where an outlet is nearby; if an extension cord is essential, run it only along the wall.

• Furniture should be color-contrasted with the floor and wall colors to demarcate edges for anyone with low vision.

• You should be able to reach a telephone easily from the comfortable chair you most favor for relaxing.

• Windows should be easy to open for good air circulation and cross ventilation; a stuffy room is an unhealthy room, most particularly for guests and family members who might not be accustomed to slightly warmer rooms.

• The room temperature should be adjustable on a separate zone control so that heat or air-conditioning can be economically supplied to only the living area.

• Keep at least a three- to four-foot uncluttered walking path through each room.

ACTIVITIES: Professional designers and even medical professionals tell us that one of the most important components of smart-aging design is the requirement that space be provided for "activities," and this doesn't mean making pot holders! Seniors are living longer every year, and not merely as sprouted couch potatoes. Both physically and intellectually, older adults are maintaining a growing array of challenging interests. If you are now an elder designing your own home, you may think you can safely ignore the necessity of space for a treadmill, a woodworking shop, or a bank of computers and peripherals, but don't count on it.

A second bedroom or a spare bedroom is a wonderful luxury for anyone interested in keeping open their options. It can, of course, always be used for guests or caregivers, but it also offers great promise as a room in which to expand your interests, however modest they may be at their inception. There are many seniors, for example, who, having been told by their grandchildren that handwritten letters were thoroughly passé, bought a computer just to send E-mail—they then became graying geeks and the envy of their peers.

As a prior generation learned to use the new-fangled telephone in their later years, it is entirely probable that many seniors will recognize the benefits of using a home computer and want to provide a comfor-

Computer center with supportive seating, task lighting, and a sleep sofa for overnight guests.

table space for a computer center. The possibilities of instantaneous and inexpensive communications with folks the world over, the chat lines, the special-interest groups, not to mention the option of paying bills and managing personal business chores from your own desk—these all are compelling reasons that elders are increasingly becoming committed computer users. Many seniors, in fact, have found that they can operate a home business with a computer, fax, and modem; the supplemental income during retirement is especially welcome.

A study undertaken in 1995 indicates that more than 30 percent of adults over fifty-five have a computer; similar studies in the next several years will surely show a dramatic increase in this percentage. The Internet is not only an excellent way to communicate with the world, but also an inexhaustible reference library that can be built into your home, purchased for less than one thousand dollars. Training sessions on how to use the computer are held in senior centers all over the country by Senior Net, as well as many other organizations, such as adult education centers.

Wherever you set up your computer center, pay attention to the lighting because glare on the monitor makes it very difficult to use. The most appropriate lighting is adjustable light on either side of the screen, because overhead light increases glare. Look for adjustable desk lamps with parabolic or louvre lenses that shield and direct the light source. Full-spectrum or chromalux bulbs are ideal to use, as they create less glare. Select the computer chair for its ergonomic design, and be sure the desk or at least the tray for the keyboard is adjustable. A good resource for home office furniture is Reliable Home Office; IKEA and The Home Depot are others.

You may not have a den or spare bedroom, but if space permits, you can set up an activity area in the living room. One of the advantages of older age is the time available to pursue hobbies or discover new interests that were not easily accommodated during one's career years. An essential practicality for any hobby or interest, though, is a place to put away or store the accompanying paraphernalia. Evaluate what tools or implements your hobby might entail, whether it's knitting, puzzles, fly-tying or merely reading; adequate storage will make the activity that much more enjoyable. A wall storage unit is ideal where space is sufficient; an armoire or a closet are other alternatives. Hanging wall shelves provide handy storage where floor space is limited.

Consider, too, what kind of electrical outlets are required, and add them if necessary so that hazardous extension cords are not necessary. Surface-mounted cable can be installed along the baseboard without any construction effort at all. You will find that electrical outlets mounted eighteen inches to thirty inches above the floor are more easily accessible than those at baseboard level.

A sturdy card table is a useful working surface for any number of activities and obviously ideal for games of all kinds. If card playing is a favorite, be certain that direct lighting over the table is sufficient and that you don't have to drag chairs across lamp cords. Playing-card holders are useful if you tire of holding cards in place or if arthritis makes arranging them difficult. Other games are available, such as puzzles with large pieces and crosswords with giant letters and other features that make them "elder friendly." These often stimulate memory and are ideal for group activity.

If you watch TV, place it in a location free from glare or reflected light. Never position the TV in front of a window, because the contrast between natural light and the electronic image can be disturbing even for those with perfect eyesight. A remote control with large numbers is helpful, as is a screen enlarger or a closed-caption TV device that provides the equivalent of subtitles to compensate for poor hearing. Another helpful item to keep handy is a magnifying glass that television viewers always enjoy—not for watching the TV but for reading the TV listings that are universally printed in maddeningly minuscule type.

An organized desk space with cubbyholes or files will go a long way to reducing clutter in the living area; for anyone who keeps up active correspondence, it will also make letter writing more enjoyable. But whether it's for bill paying or sending postcards, any activity at a desk requires bright task-lighting directed specifically at the desk surface, not just overhead or background lighting.

If you have a small kitchen or prefer to eat in front of a television in the living room, buy a wheelcart to transport the food and utensils more conveniently.

Finally, the nonactivity activity that nearly all of us most enjoy—a quiet afternoon nap—is something that should be thought of when designing the living area. A comfortable sofa with soft pillows is always inviting, or a recliner chair, though an assistive rising device should be considered if the chair tips back at a steep angle. In either case, it's nice to have the blinds on a remote control so that when a nap seems most appealing, you don't have to jump up to shut out bright afternoon light. Many elders sleep less in the evening and actually require a daytime nap to keep fit. In certain parts of the world, this time-honored custom dictates that business and social activity shut down for a few afternoon hours each day; you should have no reservations about creating a similar, siesta-friendly living environment.

LIGHTING: The lighting in any room is critical to comfort, but it's an area often not well understood by designers who have not studied the special lighting requirements of older adults. Pay attention to both natural light and artificial light; enhancing both will improve the appearance of the living room and increase your ability to enjoy it.

Natural light is always preferable to a dark, dingy room, but too much of even this good thing can cause a glare problem. Sheer curtains will reduce glare, whereas blinds provide adjustable light and total elimination of streetlight or headlights at night. Both can be bothersome.

When placing lamps around the room, be certain that they have opaque, light-colored shades to eliminate glare and that they can be easily turned off or on. A device called "touch-turn-on" can turn any lamp into one with the equivalent of a three-way bulb; wattage is automatically turned up when any metal part of the lamp is touched. You don't have to worry about grasping for chains or pulling at strings. A sensor light switch can activate all the lights in the room when you enter it. It is far safer than having to cross a dark room and grope for a lamp.

Background lighting can also be supplied by overhead fixtures, but any area where you plan to read or do close work such as sewing requires task lighting, or very direct lighting. Glare from this type of lighting is often reflected in glossy surfaces such as highly polished tables, so cover these with a tablecloth or runner. Light-colored walls will reflect light without glare and generally are good choices to "lighten up" a room without the use of artificial light or even one with limited natural light.

Most important of all, remember to keep the lighting levels uniform throughout the room. Attention to this rule eliminates dark, shadowy areas that can present a falling or tripping zone for anyone with vision problems. One attractive technique is to add a torchère in the corner of the room. This type of tall floor lamp directs most of its light to the ceiling, creating indirect room lighting that reduces glare.

CHAPTER 5

Gardens and Outdoor Spaces

IF YOU are fortunate enough to have your own garden or private outdoor space, there is no need to forego the pleasures of such a treasure as you grow older. But remember, not every access to the outdoors is a safe one; steep stairs or uneven paving stones can present very common obstacles for anyone but a sure-footed mountain goat. To maximize the use of your garden, you should ensure that access to and from the outdoors is made safe and hazard free.

It is important to acknowledge that outdoor spaces often incorporate certain environmental hazards for elders, such as cracked pavement, that can precipitate falls. Hazards must be addressed before the space can be made as comfortable and safe as elder-friendly interiors.

Transition from
Indoors to Outdoors

If you are fortunate enough to have your own outdoor living space, you should take advantage of it every moment you can. But getting in and out of the house safely can pose difficulties for many older adults, so it is important to focus on stairs, ramps, or pathways that take you from the house to the outdoors. Their construction, lighting, and maintenance are all important to the overall safety of both residents and guests in your house.

STAIRS: Try to avoid designing any area that has only one small step; several stairs are actually safer because they are more obvious; a gently sloping walkway is even better. Different-sized steps are also dangerous because they interrupt the natural rhythm of anyone's gait. If you are installing new stairs, design them so they are uniform. Handrails should be installed on both sides of the stairs; handrails not only help steady your balance when walking down slippery or wet stairs, but also add leverage when ascending the stairs. The handrail should be 1½-inches round or oval for easy gripping, installed at a height thirty-three to thirty-six inches from the top of the step.

It is best not to have nosing on the edge of the treads, since it is easy to catch a foot in it. Open risers are equally dangerous and should all be closed off. People with walkers or severe mobility problems often find that a four-inch height for the riser is easier to maneuver than the standard seven-inch height. Similarly, a larger tread (eighteen to thirty-four inches) instead of the standard eleven inches will allow the base of the walker to rest on a single stair. These enlarged dimensions are expensive to build,

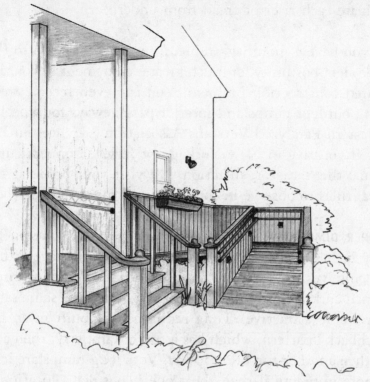

An accessible ramp can be designed for both beauty and
safety: features include nonslip flooring, handrails,
and light fixtures for nighttime use.

however, and require considerable space; unless there are only a few stairs, it may be wiser to install a ramp. An occupational therapist can offer other useful design suggestions for accommodating mobility aids in problematic areas if you are undecided about the advisability of a ramp or a staircase.

Because stairs can be dangerous in their own right, lighting becomes all the more important. Ideally, extra lighting should be supplied wherever there is a change in the surface level, both indoors and out. In the garden or on outdoor staircases, lighting can be installed to automatically illuminate when darkness falls and automatically shut off at dawn or at a preset time each night. There are even more effective lighting installations that illuminate each riser or tread from underneath.

RAMPS: If you have a mobility problem, installing a ramp to the outdoors may provide an opportunity for much greater enjoyment in your life. It is not a complicated construction problem. You can even receive free assistance in designing outdoor ramps and interior passageways for wheelchair access from the Eastern Paralyzed Veterans Association (see "Resource Guide" on page 177). If you live in New York, New Jersey, Connecticut, or eastern Pennsylvania, this same organization will visit your home at no cost.

General rules to observe in constructing a ramp include the following:

- **PROPER DIMENSIONS:** The maximum slope is one inch for every twenty inches in length, since most older adults have difficulty pushing themselves up anything steeper; forty-two-inch minimum width; four-inch curb along both sides (planters serve the same safety purpose and are more attractive). Long ramps can be built in an L-shape or a "switchback" pattern, which has a run of rampway, then a 180-degree turn, then another run of rampway. Very long ramps are less attractive and more impractical than short ones; consider a location that is not as prominent as the front of the house if possible when your setback or your lot slope requires a very long ramp.
- **CONSTRUCTION MATERIALS:** Poured concrete or pressure treated lumber; concrete is more expensive but will last longer and requires less maintenance. Trex, a comparatively new synthetic material, is another good choice because it requires no maintenance. It has the appearance of wood but is coated with a nonslip finish.
- **LANDING AREAS:** Five feet of landing space at both top and bottom is ideal; if the ramp changes directions or if the rise is more than three feet, there should be an intermediate landing.
- **SURFACE MATERIAL:** Use a nonslip deck paint on wood ramps; concrete can be brushed with a broom while wet to create better traction; a textured surface on both the top and bottom of the ramp will serve as a location cue for the visually impaired.

- **RAILINGS ON RAMP:** There should be two railings, one at thirty-six inches for walking, one at twenty-eight inches for wheelchairs.
- Before constructing a ramp, check with the building code office in your community to see whether a building permit is required.
- Order a manual on how to build ramps that includes detailed drawings by sending ten dollars to the Metropolitan Center for Independent Living, 1600 University Avenue West, St. Paul, MN 55104-3825; 612-646-8342.
- Portable ramps can also be installed in spaces where the slope is steep, especially when the need for a wheelchair is seen as temporary; but a caregiver must be present at all times to assist. Steeply sloped ramps cannot be negotiated safely alone by most older adults who use wheelchairs. Wheelchair platforms and other specialized electrical equipment can be installed as well.

PATHWAYS AND WALKWAYS: If you are fortunate enough to have the space for walkways in your garden, be certain that they are safe enough to enjoy. The surface should be as even as possible, and any cracks or stumbling hazards should be patched to prevent falls. It's both visually appealing and safe to add colorful flowers, clearly marking the edges of the walkway. If the area is used at night, install solar lighting that needs no electrical connections and comes on automatically at dusk. In climates with limited sun, use low-voltage lighting. You can apply the same design ideas to pathways that lead from the street to your entrance, or from the garage to the back door.

Walkways should be at least three feet wide, but a wider path, forty-eight to fifty-four inches, gives two people the opportunity to walk side by side. If the weather in your area is often rainy or icy, take care when selecting a surface material for the walkways. Colored concrete, brick, or wood composite are excellent choices. Pressure-treated wood resists rot from ground contact and should be used for construction supports in the ground; the surface of a wooden walkway requires a penetrating stain applied. Small spaces left between boards will help drainage and delay weather damage.

DECKS: Most decks are built adjacent to the house, with sliding doors connecting to the interior of the house. Depending on your site, it's also possible to build a low-level deck, raised only slightly off the ground, with a gentle sloping ramp for access. If you are thinking about building a new deck, first decide on the best location, free standing or adjoining the house, then think about orientation toward the sun and the best view. Size is the next consideration. Remember to leave space for outdoor furniture and, if space permits, a table for eating. Then choose the type of material you want to use. The same considerations appropriate to wooden walkways apply to decks. Pressure-treated wood should be used for in-ground posts, but attractive heartwoods (redwood, cedar, and cypress) that are naturally rot and insect resistant can be used for flooring.

Trex is a new material recently introduced for outdoor construction projects. Its advantages are that it looks like wood and is maintenance free; made entirely of recycled materials such as plastics, scrapwood, and sawdust, without any chemical preservatives, it is environmentally sound. Its surface is pebbly textured and therefore nonslip. Depending on the costs of lumber in your area, you may find that Trex is slightly more expensive than pressure-treated wood, but in the long run the advantages will outweigh the cost.

Understand the building codes in your area before you plan your deck's railing. The perimeter of a deck can be beautifully landscaped with planter boxes, but even this design feature will be regulated by the code, so check before you build.

PATIOS: Patios are wonderful outdoor spaces because if properly designed they also have a sense of intimacy, even when they open onto a large yard. Create this coziness by adding "living walls" of trellised plants or flowering shrubs. Depending on how the patio is sited, you may want to add a roof overhang or an arbor that gives you a choice of shade or full sun. In climates where outdoor living is problematic, an indoor patio can be a sensible substitute; large windows and skylights can provide the sense of being cozily ensconced and at the same time outdoors in the beauty of a natural setting. If you want to be able to use an indoor patio or sunroom

Cushioned chairs, shading from the sun, and an accessible garden add to the pleasures of the outdoors.

all year, be sure it incorporates adequate climate controls. Tinted windows will reduce glare, and outdoor awnings will shade the windows from bright summer sun. While manual awnings can be difficult to roll up and down, Durasol awnings are electrically operated and can be rolled up or down as easily as turning on a lightswitch. Be sure to check building codes for lot restrictions and for underground utilities before starting any construction.

Most outdoor patio floors are either brick or cement. Any surface that is smooth is a good choice, but handmade tiles or rocks, because they are designed to be nonuniform, are inappropriate. If you choose brick, be sure the joint spaces are minimal; anything more than one-quarter inch between bricks makes a dangerous, uneven surface. Choose bricks that are right for your climate; otherwise, cracks will develop from the repeated cycle of freezing and thawing.

Concrete can be an excellent choice, with far more imaginative textures and colors available than you might realize. A textured surface can be created by sandblasting, troweling, or mixing small pebbles into the top layer. To color concrete, you can either mix pigments into the entire batch of dry white cement or color just the top inch. Soft shades or adobe-type colors are especially attractive.

If your patio is being built to adjoin your living room or another room in the house, be certain that the sill is no more than one-quarter inch. This sill can easily accommodate a sliding glass door.

FRONT PORCH: The classic front porch is an American institution, one that provides a degree of privacy while offering the opportunity to take part in community life. It also serves the practical purpose of providing shelter when you are searching for your keys in bad weather or when visitors ring the bell on a snowy evening.

The perfect porch is built wide enough to accommodate several chairs and a table, plus extra seating for visitors. Screened porches are essential in some climates if they are to be used at all on hot summer evenings. Be sure to add good lighting on both sides of the porch or under the overhang, so that you needn't step from a well-lit area into a dark one or vice versa. The front porch should also include shelving beside the door so that when you or others approach laden with packages, there is a convenient place to set them down.

Gardens

If you are passionate about gardening, you know that there is never enough time to accomplish what you would like. Retirement is the best thing that could ever happen to a serious gardener; elders find that finally they are free to devote much more time to their plants than merely the essential weekend upkeep. But the best advice any ambitious gardener can follow is to simplify the entire garden design. Let "low maintenance" be your mantra, and keep the following list of indisputable facts nailed to your garden shed:

1. High-maintenance lawn is NOT the only attractive ground cover.
2. There are magnificent annuals that require constant care, and many perennials that reseed themselves year after year; choose from the latter group.
3. Automatic or sensor watering systems will free you forever from a rigid watering schedule.
4. Low-maintenance materials are just as easy to install and as pleasing as high-maintenance materials.
5. Raised beds and container gardens will save you and your back hours of strenuous labor.
6. Mulch, mulch, mulch.

Even if you have large, open garden areas that you don't want cluttered with shrubs or trees, grass is not your only choice. Ground covers include perennials, herbs, shrubs, sprawling vines, mosses, and low-growing plants such as ivy and daisies. These plants are not only low or no maintenance, but also provide much more textural variation than a flat expanse of lawn. If you know the type of soil you have and the amount of sun or shade the area gets in each season, your local nursery can advise you on a number of low-maintenance options. Why worry about cutting the grass each week (and maintaining the mower) when you could be sitting on your porch, looking out over a field of periwinkle?

Many ground covers such as heather or vibrantly colored trailing ice plants can withstand constant sun and are even forgiving of drought. From a design perspective, scale is the governing principle; if your garden is small, choose a ground cover such as ajuga, which has tiny leaves and pink or white flowers in the spring. Larger areas can support large-scaled plants such as moss phlox or dwarf spreading honeysuckle.

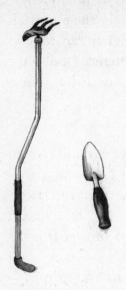

Ergonomic garden tools.

Gardening can be enjoyed at any age as long as the backbreaking labor is eliminated. Garden tools have been redesigned by many different companies so that less bending and reaching are necessary; handles have been constructed on many smaller tools so that they are easier to hold, even for those with arthritis. In most climates, there are so many plants to choose from that once a perennial garden is planted, it should offer years of beauty with little care, assuming that low-maintenance systems are in place.

Watering is a major time consumer for gardeners, but rather than waste hours standing in your garden with a hose or waste water with a sprinkler system that lets only 50 percent of the water reach the plants and the other 50 percent evaporate, select a drip irrigation system. A tube with tiny pinholes is laid along the ground, concealed under mulch or shrubs.

Kneeler/Seat provides cushioning for the knees, handles for getting up and down, and a place to sit when turned over.

When the faucet is turned on, the water slowly seeps directly into the root system where it is most useful. Any drip system can be connected to an electronic water timer that automatically waters the garden on a seven-day schedule up to four times a day.

If you have areas that cannot practically be reached with a drip system, or ones you choose to water manually, buy a lightweight hose of rubber and vinyl. These hoses are 50 percent lighter than standard hoses and infinitely easier to drag around.

CONTAINER GARDENING

Even if your outdoor space is limited, gardening is an activity you can still pursue. There are myriad ways to garden in containers and pots that add beauty to your surroundings. Small containers are portable, so as the seasons change, they can be moved to an area that gets the best conditions, thereby extending the growing season. With container gardens, you also eliminate gardening on your knees.

Planters come in an infinite number of sizes, shapes, and materials; take advantage of the diversity to create a dramatic visual impact. Stone is the most expensive material, but there are many less costly fiberglass imitations that create an almost identical look. Terra-cotta and earthenware pots must be kept dry during the winter to prevent damage, so consider less fragile pots if you live in a climate with frigid winters. If you choose wood, be sure the container walls are at least two inches thick for support: Soil is heavy.

Sensor water containers have a reservoir that needs to be filled only once every four to six weeks. Moisture is released as it is required. You can choose from boxes large enough to hold a tree or small enough to sit on the windowsill. Whatever the size or shape of the container, be certain the potting soil you use to fill it is suited to the particular plant. Your nursery can guide you on this choice and tell you whether there is sufficient space for the root system to take hold properly within the container.

PLANTER BOXES: Ready-made boxes of durable composite products can be bought in different lengths. A planter box between twenty-four and forty inches high is ideal; you needn't bend far in order to work in it, and it can be used to create easily visible borders on walkways, decks, or patios. Some boxes are made with a twelve-inch ledge that allows you to sit and garden at the same time. In a deep planter box such as this, be sure to add a four-inch layer of rocks at the bottom before adding soil, to ensure proper drainage.

Shallow boxes for windowsills ordinarily have built-in drainage systems. Some come with sensor watering devices that indicate when moisture is required; this feature is important on window boxes because excess water can seep into walls and cause structural damage. Some planters fit snugly on deck railings; these add a beautiful touch of color at eye level when you are seated.

VERTICAL, HANGING, OR TABLETOP GARDENS

Popular in Europe for decades, vertical gardens—those that do not require vast acreage but grow up rather than horizontally—are now becoming more common in North America. There are a number of different designs for growing vegetables or vines in small spaces that are ideal for elders who aren't interested in stooping and bending all morning to pull weeds. Trellises and bamboo teepee kits are available from catalogs; they can support many varieties of climbing plants and even vegetables and fruit such as tomatoes. If you have a fence with good soil beneath it, this, too, is a ready-made, easily reachable support for your vertical garden.

Hanging wire baskets are an ideal way to bring the natural beauty of flowers to a height that is often more apparent than at ground level. You can line a wire basket with moist moss, then fill it with potting soil that is appropriate to the type of plant you select. Phlox and begonias are very often seen in wire baskets, but strawberries, cherry tomatoes, and culinary herbs all do equally well.

If you want to do all your gardening while sitting, it is entirely possible to plant a complete vegetable garden, or any other garden, on a tabletop. Choose containers that are 24 by 36 by 8 inches with good drainage. Beets, carrots, zucchini, and onions will all do well in this much soil, as will many other plants. For purely decorative gardening, consider bonsai trees and plants. They are wonderful conversation pieces and a creative way to merge fine art with fine gardening.

ENJOYING THE GARDEN

If you want to get the most pleasure from your outdoor space at any time of day, you should think about providing areas that offer shade as well as sun. Trees provide natural shade, but if your yard has too few, consider a trellis with closely spaced boards. Plant a climbing rose beside the trellis, and as the summers come and go, you will soon be sitting under a bower of magnificent blossoms.

Umbrellas provide relatively portable shade, and some now can be purchased as part of a system in which the umbrella fits in the center of a lightweight table. This gives you the option of eating outside in shady comfort or of bringing your handicraft projects outside to work on. As often as not, these tables are white plastic, but the color choice is troublesome because it can create glare. Buy a vinyl tablecloth that is a bright, but pleasing color and weight it down with a large candleholder. Even if your table has an umbrella in the center, tablecloths with zippers are designed exactly for this situation.

Choose outdoor furniture with care because uncomfortable seating space will keep you and your guests from enjoying the garden to its fullest. There are basically four different construction materials used for garden furniture: wood, wrought iron, plastic, and lightweight aluminum. Wood and wrought iron are generally the most attractive choices, but not necessarily the most comfortable except with well-padded cushioning. Both are relatively heavy and, therefore, not easy to move, but they are stable due to the weight and won't blow about in high winds.

Aluminum and plastic are generally the lightest weight choices and, therefore, the most portable. Relatively inexpensive, these materials are mostly impervious to the elements. But oftentimes, too, they are comparatively flimsy, so make sure you choose furniture that is sturdy enough to support your weight. If anyone in your family has mobility problems and often leans on stable objects for balance, lightweight furniture is a poor choice, however portable or inexpensive. It tips easily and, therefore, presents constant danger.

Part of the enjoyment of a garden is derived from the quiet privacy and peace it can provide. If these are lacking for any reason, much of your pleasure in the garden will be diminished.

You can control noise by landscaping with trees, but unless you're willing to pay the price for planting large, mature trees, you should think about adding a berm. This is a raised mound of earth, generally three feet high at its maximum point, with gently sloping sides; it can be formed wherever necessary to block and absorb street noise. Additional privacy can be created with lattice walls, vine-covered wire fencing, or ordinary wooden fencing. You don't want to add privacy at the cost of ventilation though, so use open fencing if you live in a climate where breezes are an important source of relief from hot, muggy air.

THE BIRDS, THE BEES, AND THE BUGS

If you enjoy watching wildlife, you might want to dedicate a small section of your yard to plants that invite visiting birds and butterflies. Place flowering plants and bird feeders in full sun if possible and where they can be seen from the house. Butterflies and hummingbirds are attracted to bee balm, scarlet sage, and a variety of other plants. Ask your local nursery for suggestions for your particular climate.

Insects clearly do their part in Mother Nature's overall scheme; however, it is hard to think charitably toward them if they are also eating you alive. The most natural and often the most effective way to control insects is to introduce a colony of their predators. Birds are voracious insect consumers, and you should invite as many as possible to your garden with feeders, treehouses, or their favorite, red berry shrubs. Bats are equally if not more effective for insect control, eating three times their weight in bugs each night. Bats have a poor reputation, but it is one that is largely undeserved; during mosquito season you will congratulate yourself for having had the foresight to provide bat lodging. Specially designed bat houses are made to hang in residential gardens.

You can always find refuge, of course, on a well-screened porch, and in some climates, there is no better place to pass an August evening. If you already have a porch, new screening systems are available that are both inexpensive and easy to install. Screen Tight is a product that uses a spline method of screening as opposed to the traditional stapled wood lattice technique. The screen is folded into a base strip that is then capped securely into place; you can have your own bug-free universe within a matter of hours.

CHAPTER 6

The Smart-Aging Bedroom

FOR MANY of us—those with a studio apartment, those with a preference for small and intimate spaces, or even for the self-confessed couch potato—the bedroom often becomes our universe by choice. Properly designed, the bedroom can represent the luxury of a comfortable, welcoming living area, a place where seniors can visit with family members away from other activities in the house, eat meals relaxing in front of the television, read the morning papers, or simply meditate in the quite serenity of a comfortable setting. When designing a smart-aging bedroom, each separate activity that might be pursued requires a thoughtful analysis of practicality and aesthetic content.

Consider the different "viewpoints" the room must have to accommodate your needs. Begin by simply asking yourself how the room is used.

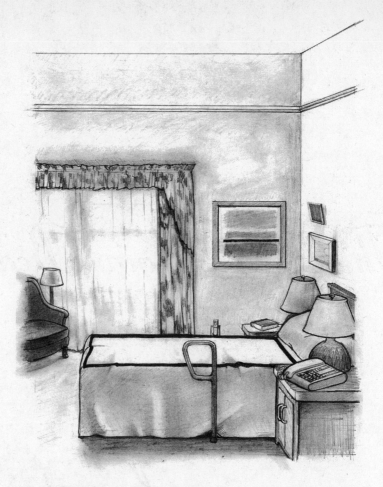

The design of a smart-aging bedroom includes a supportive mattress and chair, a bedrail to make getting in and out of bed easier, and a sensor night-light.

● Do you use the bedroom merely as a place to sleep, or do you also consider it a second living room, a place to visit with friends and family away from other activities in the house?

● Do you have enough space to eat meals, watch TV, or exercise in your bedroom, and if so, is it properly equipped for all these activities?

● Have you paid close enough attention to smart-aging design details that will enable you to enjoy your bedroom in your seventies or eighties?

The Bedroom as a Place to Spend Leisure Time

The bedroom that is designed for more than just sleeping can be a wonderful place to visit with guests who stop by to share the neighborhood news or perhaps a cup of tea. But is the room as comfortable for visitors as for those living in it? We all enjoy the presence of a friend or loved one merely being in the room; seniors, particularly those in recuperation, will often have their spirits lifted by the presence of someone else in the room even if they are dozing. Why not make the space as accommodating as possible for visitors?

DESIGN ELEMENTS FOR BEDROOM LEISURE

● **CHAIRS:** Select chairs with firm seats and solid supporting arms, to provide assistance when rising from the chair. Avoid low or deep chairs because both features make rising more difficult. Some chairs are made with an "automated rising device" that can assist people with diminished leg strength.

● **THOUGHTFUL LIGHTING:** Place a high-intensity reading lamp beside a comfortable chair or between a pair of chairs. Floor lamps should have long string pulls or easily accessible toggles. A new device called "touch-turn-on" can turn any lamp into a three-way lamp; wattage is automatically turned up when any metal part of the lamp is touched. No grasping or pulling at strings is required.

Touch-turn adapter.

● **ATTENTION TO NATURAL LIGHT:** Strong afternoon sun can cause glare and discomfort. Sheer curtains reduce glare, whereas blinds provide adjustable light and eliminate the light from streetlights at night.

● **READING AIDS:** Keep a magnifying glass on the table beside your reading chair. It is always a thoughtful gesture and a handy visual aid for all ages.

● **AVAILABLE STORAGE:** Provide bookcases or other furniture to store books, knitting, or other hobby items, so they are easily accessible but don't create obstacles on the floor or clutter on other surfaces. Hanging wall shelves provide additional storage where floor space is limited.

● **ELECTRICAL OUTLETS:** The ability to plug in small appliances or additional lamps is important for the enjoyment of leisure in a bedroom. Installing multiple outlets on all walls prevents the need to run potentially dangerous extension cords. Surface-mounted cable can be installed along the baseboard without any construction effort at all. Electrical outlets mounted eighteen to thirty inches above the floor are more accessible than those at baseboard level.

● **BEDSIDE TELEPHONE:** Every bedroom should have a phone with large easy-to-read buttons that light in the dark. A speakerphone may also be more comfortable for some elders, but cordless phones, which are easily misplaced, are not recommended for those tending toward forgetfulness.

● **BED-READING PILLOW:** Designed to support the back, neck, and shoulders in an upright position, these pillows are a much healthier choice than the bunching and stacking of soft down pillows for reading in bed.

● **VIEWS FROM THE BED:** Whether this is a room you're creating for yourself or someone else, you won't know what is seen from the bed until you lie on it and look out—and up. If you're flat on your back, it's nice to have ceiling art—restful colors, a flower-covered trellis perhaps. Prone or upright, you should consider what will be seen from the bed, whether light is shining in your eyes at certain times of the day, or whether the most important item in the room, such as grandchildren's artwork, is easily visible.

The Bedroom as a Place to Dress

Closet design has become a very significant concern to home builders in recent years, and new homeowners have discovered the luxury of having spacious closets that can be quickly and easily organized. Those of us living in older buildings are all too familiar with the necessity of stepladders, flashlights, and considerable patience when searching the bedroom closet. Designing a smart-aging bedroom requires special attention to closet space that if not well thought out can present major obstacles for elders.

DESIGN ELEMENTS FOR A BEDROOM TO DRESS IN

- **WALK-IN/ROLL-IN CLOSET:** The ideal closet has five feet of unobstructed floor space for potential wheelchair access.
- **CLOSET LIGHTING:** Install lighting that is automatically turned on when the door is opened. This feature can be wired in with new construction, or a battery-powered unit can be added with less effort to existing closets.
- **WIRE CLOSET SYSTEMS:** Easy to install, these component-part systems allow the best possible design, with a rod at a suitable height on one side of the closet and sliding shelves or drawers on the other.

- **OPEN FLOOR SPACE:** The customary clutter of too many shoes on the closet floor invites accidents and causes more bending and reaching than necessary; install a shoe bag on the inside of the closet door.
- **DRESSERS AND ARMOIRES:** Be sure that drawers are not bulky; if they stick when pulled, rub the slides with a bar of soap. This will make opening and closing them much smoother. Roller glides can also be installed on heavy or particularly cumbersome drawers, depending on the construction of the furniture.
- **DRAWER PULLS AND HANDLES:** Easily grasped C handles are the most comfortable for anyone and especially for those with restricted hand agility.

Be realistic about what is frequently used and what is not. Anything that you don't use every day but still want to keep should be stored on the higher, less-accessible shelves. And what is *never* used qualifies only as clutter; donate it to charity, or if it's too worn, throw it out.

The Bedroom as a Place to Exercise

When mobility is restricted, it does not necessarily follow that an elder is unable to exercise or is uninterested in exercise. And the more convenient it is to take modest exercise in the bedroom, the more inviting is the opportunity to do so. Many common physical ailments that once were thought to be an inevitable feature of the aging process are now recognized more commonly as the results of a sedentary lifestyle. The benefits of even modest exercise are many: development of greater bone density, which reduces the risk of osteoporosis; increased endurance, strength, and balance; and even the reduction of mental or physical pain.

Strength Training for People 80 to 90 Years Old

At the Hebrew Rehabilitation Center for the Aged, Dr. Maria Fiatarone designed an exercise program for a group of the nursing home's residents, all of whom were in their eighties and nineties. The objective was to build progressive resistance strength training for hip and knee muscles. After only ten weeks of professionally supervised training, three times a week for forty-five minutes, participants were found to have increased their muscle strength by 113 percent. There was, on average, a 12 percent increase in walking speed, and a 28 percent increase in stair-climbing power.

New products and new fitness guides have been developed by several companies for seniors, but unless some space in the bedroom (or elsewhere) is thoughtfully designed for safe, modest exercise, it is too easy to ignore the challenge of making exercise a part of one's normal routine. Older adults who are infirm or recuperating also require physical movement; especially in situations where the patient is frail, safety concerns are of paramount importance. The smart-aging bedroom should be designed to ensure that, at a minimum, the patient is able to rise from bed and is able to walk with assurance around the room and to the bathroom.

DESIGN ELEMENTS FOR MODEST
EXERCISE IN THE BEDROOM

- **SAFE FLOORING:** Remove any high-gloss shine and replace it with matte finish. It is much less slippery.

Equipment Availability

Equipment should be easily accessible, but stored off the floor, where it might present a hazard. Consider the following options:

- *Thera-Band and Ball:* Stretchable rubber strips to improve strength and range of motion; easy to use with variable resistance.

- *Exercise Putty:* To improve hand strength and dexterity.

- *Bicycle Pedals (without the rest of the bike):* Can be used from a standard chair or a wheelchair; excellent for increased circulation and leg strength, or even for upper body workouts, pedaling with hands.

- *Vinyl-covered Dumbbells:* Easier to grip than metal.

- *Cuff Weights:* Attached to legs or arms with Velcro; no manual grip strength is required.

- **AREA RUGS:** These are not advisable because, unless securely tacked with double-edged tape, they can create hazards and cause falls.
- **CARPETING:** Carpets with a biological guard and a nonflow-through plastic backing are ideal in minimizing the damage from spilled medicine, food, or other liquids.
- **SHAG CARPETS:** Shag carpets are inadvisable because tripping is a constant hazard with this type of floor covering. The same advantages of coziness, sound absorption, and reduced heat loss can be achieved with low-pile carpeting.
- **HANDRAILS:** Easily added to long walls in the bedroom, hallway, or elsewhere, these supports, properly screwed into the wall studs, can assist in building self-confidence for the frail and add an incomparable measure of safety. The rails should be installed at a height of thirty-three to thirty-six inches from the floor. One company, Crest Elec-

tronics, Inc., has a 1½-inch round handrail made of aluminum with a textured nylon finish. It is available in twenty decorator colors, economically priced, and shipped by UPS in six-foot lengths.

The Bedroom as a Place to Sleep

A quiet, restful night of sleep is restorative at any age, but especially important to seniors. It enhances an overall sense of well-being and promotes healing for those in recuperation. The National Institute on Aging, however, finds that changes in our circadian rhythms often interfere with our ability to sleep well as we age, and if one partner is tossing about in bed, it can be disruptive to the partner who might otherwise be able to sleep soundly. Separate beds are one solution to this problem, but often other changes such as a new mattress will make peaceful sleep more accessible to both partners. Some research indicates that such simple changes as scenting a room with lavender can aid some older adults in sleeping restfully, even to the extent of ending the need for sleeping medication. But of the many elements that promote a quiet night's sleep, the most important consideration of all is surely the comfort of the bed.

DESIGN ELEMENTS FOR THE SLEEPING BEDROOM

- **RISING FROM BED:** This often difficult task can be measurably eased by the installation of a handrail, adjustable in height, attachable to the bedframe without tools, capable of both swiveling and locking in place.
- **BEDSIDE TABLE AND LAMP:** The table should be generously sized with rounded corners and a raised lip around the edge to prevent items from sliding off. The lamp must be easy to reach, with a three-

way bulb and an on-off switch that can be easily managed even if fine motor skills are lessened, making small switches troublesome.

● **NIGHT-LIGHTS:** Automatic night-lights as well as illuminated light switches at the bedroom door make late-night visits to the bathroom much safer.

● **BED HEIGHT:** The user's feet should touch the floor when he or she is seated on the bed; if not, cut the bed frame down or buy a shorter metal base from a bedding company. (Frames measuring three inches or seven inches from the floor are available.) Wheelchairs are eighteen inches high, and a frame three inches from the floor will make a bed roughly the same height, easing transfer from bed to chair.

● **ELECTRIC BEDS:** The versatility of electric beds makes them well suited to a variety of medical conditions. Isolated areas of the bed can be raised so that circulatory problems, for example, can be eased, with a heightened foot, and breathing disorders comforted by raising the upper portion of the bed.

● **ORTHOPEDIC NECK PILLOW:** These support the natural curve of the upper spine and are generally more effective than ordinary pillows for those with neck or back pain.

● **BACK PILLOW:** These thick support pillows of open-cell foam are designed for placement under the lower back to relieve pressure points and support the spine in its natural position.

● **MATTRESS:** Contrary to conventional wisdom, a firm mattress is rarely ideal for elders. Too often it can exacerbate aching shoulders, back, or neck. Coil spring mattresses generally have a product life of only ten years, and older lumpy mattresses can cause many sleepless nights. New product introductions have greatly enhanced the choices in mattress selection, and if you're shopping for a new one, don't hesitate to simply lie down on the beds and let individual comfort dictate your selection. Consider these choices:

● *Metal Coil Mattress:* These mattresses are available in different "strengths." Always choose one that keeps your spinal column properly aligned. If your current mattress is too hard, you may awake feeling pressure around your hips or shoulder area. Lower back pain, on the other hand, may indicate a mattress that is too soft.

• *Air Mattress:* Research conducted at the University of London indicates air mattresses exert 25 percent less pressure on the body than conventional innerspring mattresses. This is particularly important in lessening the likelihood of bedsores for those requiring prolonged bed rest. Certain brands of air mattresses provide controls to adjust the degree of firmness on only one side of the mattress, much like an electric blanket with dual controls.

• *Open-cell Foam Mattress:* Often used in nursing homes, hospitals, and sleep clinics, these mattresses are conducive to less tossing and turning for many who have difficulty sleeping. Open-cell mattresses distribute the body's pressure evenly over the entire surface, and in many cases can reduce aches and pains in the hip, back, and shoulder area.

• *Mattress Overlay Pad:* Excellent for relieving pressure, without incurring the costs of a new mattress. Avoid standard, flat foam that will compress, and buy one made of open-cell foam, textured foam (like an egg carton), or one filled with air. The pad is placed directly on top of the existing mattress and will add approximately one inch to the bed height. This should be considered in adjusting the height of the bed.

The Bedroom as a Place to Heal

Hospitals today are anxious to send patients home as quickly as possible, and with good reason. Evidence is very compelling that wellness is promoted in an environment that is comforting and familiar to the patient. What better environment than the patient's own bedroom. But it is important to recognize that the average bedroom is neither equipped nor suited to all the needs of a recovering patient. Both the caregiver and receiver will benefit from a systematic review of the equipment needed to speed a patient's recovery. This subject is covered in depth in the "Home Hospital" section in chapter 9 (page 144). For additional information on how to set up a bedroom for a wheelchair user, please refer to the section "Mobility Limitations," also in chapter 9 (page 114).

CHAPTER 7

The Smart-Aging Kitchen

THE KITCHEN often represents the creative heart of an emotionally nourishing family home. When reflecting on childhood, we often associate food with our fondest memories and, like Proust, are moved to profound remembrances by even the aroma of our family's traditional foods being prepared. Fast foods and take-out foods have lessened the time most families spend on meal preparation, but these conveniences have not lessened the importance of sharing a meal or, from that perspective, the significance of the kitchen itself. Whether we are merely reheating food or laboriously preparing an elaborate holiday dinner, preparing and eating meals represent an important opportunity for all of us to share our lives with others.

Such social interaction is of increasing importance as we age, though very often our ability to prepare all our own meals, or our interest in doing so, declines. A poorly designed kitchen is difficult and frustrating to work in, even for the

A smart-aging kitchen. Features include an adjustable-height sink, separate cooktop and wall oven, and accessible storage.

most dedicated, energetic cook; an older adult may find working in such an environment simply too taxing and thus lose an important opportunity to enjoy shared meals with others. Similarly, if an elder has experienced diminished physical abilities or is recuperating from illness, relying constantly on others for preparation of meals can be demeaning. A sense of self-sufficiency, productivity, and independence is fostered by being able to care for ourselves in the simplest of tasks, and surely by being able to provide our own nourishment. To this extent, a kitchen designed for smart aging will do much more than make food preparation pleasant. It will enhance the quality of your life, however long and productive it may be.

Flexibility and Adaptability of Design

It is important to think through how the kitchen is used in your own family situation and how it might logically be used in the foreseeable future. Ask yourself the following questions:

- Is one person responsible for most of the meal preparation, or do two (or more) cooks work in the kitchen simultaneously?
- What are the physical characteristics of those who use the kitchen? Different heights of individual cooks suggest different heights for work surfaces, just as different physical abilities must be considered.
- How much food is actually prepared in the kitchen? If pizza is often delivered or if frozen entrees are a frequent meal of choice, some of the kitchen space might logically be diverted to another, better use.

In planning a new kitchen or remodeling an existing one, imagine what your situation might be in fifteen or twenty years. Major renovation, however challenging at a creative level, is not a project most seventy-year-olds would willingly choose to undertake. If you intend to stay in your house as you age, then try to imagine how you would want to live in the next decade or two. If you are young and starting a new family, you may not think you need to incorporate as many elder-friendly design features as those in their retirement years. But consider that your parents may one day be using your kitchen or that an older couple may be interested in buying your house if you do decide to move.

Of course, no one can predict with certainty what their physical abilities might be in the future, and age is not the only predictor of functional ability. But the more flexibility built into a kitchen when it is designed, the less work will be required in later remodeling.

LAYOUT AND DESIGN

Regardless of the size of your kitchen, how many people you cook for, or your personal cooking habits, the general work flow in any kitchen is virtually the same. Ingredients are generally taken from the refrigerator to the sink for rinsing, then brought to the work surface, then placed in a pot on the cooktop or put into the oven. Alternatively, you take food from the freezer directly to the microwave or to the oven. Under most circumstances, an L-shaped or U-shaped kitchen is the ideal design. It should have five feet of floor space between the cabinets or the walls to accommodate wheelchairs or walkers.

The more continuous work-surface (countertop) space available, the more flexibility the cook has in preparing food. There is also less lifting and moving of heavy pots, utensils, and various ingredients. This type of arrangement enables an individual with limited upper-body strength to slide containers from one place to another with ease. Other important general criteria in smart-aging kitchen design are the following:

- **EASY APPROACH:** Oven, cooktop, and dishwasher should be placed where they can be approached from the right, left, or front, accommodating the cook's natural inclination toward left- or right-handed activity, or favoring a person's stronger physical side.
- **EFFICIENCY FOR CLEANUP:** The closer the sink is to the cooktop, the less you have to lift heavy pots and pans for cleaning.
- **CLEAR FLOOR SPACE:** There should be an area of clear floor space in front of the refrigerator, stove, cooktop, and sink measuring thirty by forty-eight inches. This space will allow a cook who uses a mobility aid much easier access. Similarly, if the kitchen design includes a table

or an island in the center, aisles should be forty-two to forty-eight inches wide.

● **CONSOLIDATED DESIGN:** Kitchens are traditionally designed around "the work triangle," which is the distance between the sink, range, and refrigerator. Long triangle legs can make meal preparation exhausting; short ones create a feeling of confinement. A good rule of thumb is that the three legs of the triangle, when added together, should not exceed twenty-two feet. If space permits, a dining table in the kitchen saves walking and reduces fatigue. Alternately, a pass-through window between the kitchen and dining area can serve the same purpose. Folding wooden shutters can camouflage the pass-through when it's not being used.

REDUCING FATIGUE AND ACCIDENTS

However satisfying meal preparation may be, it can also be tiring, given the amount of manual labor sometimes required. Fatigue coupled with a sharp butcher knife is a combination that's an accident waiting to happen. Guarding against overexertion requires attention to the following guidelines:

● Reduce physical exertion: Keep bending, lifting, and reaching to a minimum. Replace heavy iron cookware with lighter weight aluminum or stainless-steel pots and pans.

● Maintain abundant, high-quality light: Use light colors to reflect more light, and add under-cabinet, full-spectrum fluorescent lighting to provide direct lighting on work surfaces.

● Make sure there's a place to sit, either for resting between tasks or even for while you're working.

● Remember that the kitchen is the single most frequent source of fires in the home; protect against this in your own kitchen.

- Select proper flooring that is well cushioned and slip resistant; it will reduce both fatigue and the possibility of falls.
- Focus on the kitchen as the heart of the home, a social center where simple food can be prepared in a barrier-free environment, not a commissary where routinized cooking tasks are performed.

Kitchen Appliances

There was a time when the choice in kitchen appliances was limited to color and size. No longer. The array of products available is so staggering that it is often more confusing than liberating. Remember in making your appliance selections that all controls should be easy-to-touch pads or easy-to-turn dials with large lettering or numbering. In addition, color contrasting is always helpful for "older eyes." Here are some of the vast array of new appliances that are geared toward smart-aging kitchen design.

COOKTOPS AND WALL OVENS

Having a separate cooktop and wall oven is ideal because the cooktop can be set into an adjustable-height countertop, and the oven can be installed at any height on the wall to prevent bending or reaching. Both appliances should have ample set-down space on either side for hot dishes.

- Cooktops can be installed at thirty or thirty-two inches for those who might want to sit and cook, but the appliance must be insulated on the underside. Regardless of the height, the cooktop should be set into a countertop with a lip to contain spills. Automatic shutoff timers and easy-to-use touch or turn dials on the side are also useful features.
- **MAGNETIC INDUCTION COOKTOPS:** The surface of this type is not hot to the touch, yet works as effectively as gas or electric types. (Only

certain types of stainless-steel cookware can be used on these cook-tops.)

- **ELECTRIC COOKTOPS:** Select white background with black raised cast-iron circles for good color contrast. (Black coils are also acceptable, but harder to clean.)

- **RADIANT COOKTOPS OR HALOGEN COOKTOPS:** Both surfaces are smooth and turn bright red when hot, a visual aid for safety if the cook has limited eyesight. Halogen heats more quickly than radiant panels but is more expensive.

- **WALL OVENS:** Select a self-cleaning oven with either a pull-down door (ideal for putting down hot pots) or a side-opening door (suited to those in wheelchairs). A side-door selection requires installation of a heat-resistant pullout shelf under the oven to protect against spills and burns. The base of the oven should be twenty-nine to thirty-four inches above the floor.

- **RANGE HOOD ABOVE COOKTOP OR OVEN:** Consider a range hood with radius, or rounded corners, and hang it no lower than fifty-six to sixty inches from the floor. Downdraft models are recommended for grilling and frying; updraft models, for the evacuation of steam. The size and type of fan used in the hood determines the noise level, so be sure to listen to the unit you're considering in the showroom. For added safety, an automatic fire suppressant system can be purchased separately and installed into virtually any type of range hood.

MICROWAVE OVENS

Microwave ovens should be placed, like other cooking appliances, where adjacent open space allows you to set down hot dishes quickly and comfortably. If the microwave is installed under the counter, you must constantly bend over to put dishes in, then bend and lift heavy hot items out again. Some older adults are less familiar with microwaves and prefer toaster ovens, but product design has evolved dramatically, making most newer microwave models quite user-friendly. If you don't now use a microwave and don't plan to, leave a logical space at countertop level anyway, because you or another occupant might choose to install one later.

- **EASY-TO-USE MICROWAVE:** Sharp makes a model with an automatic timer and a sensor detector to shut off when food is reheated to the proper temperature. With only one button to push, it is easy to use.
- **COMBINATION MICROWAVE/CONVECTION OVEN:** All microwaves heat vegetables and potatoes efficiently, but poultry and meats often develop a rubbery consistency. A convection oven can be used for these dishes and will cook 25 percent faster than a standard oven.
- **COMBINATION MICROWAVE/CONVECTION/GRILL OVEN:** Made by KitchenAid, this appliance offers maximum flexibility for all types of food preparation.

GARBAGE AND TRASH

A garbage disposal is very helpful in reducing the amount of food waste that might otherwise need to be carried outdoors, though in some communities, building codes preclude them. To allow for knee space while sitting at the sink, locate the garbage disposal at the back of the sink or on one side of a double sink. Trash compactors won't reduce the weight of materials to be disposed of, but the volume is reduced, making the chore of carrying somewhat easier.

A good system will organize waste disposal. Consider the following ideas:

- Two different waste containers, one for garbage, one for recyclables: Place containers on pullout wire shelves, and store receptacles under the sink or in a nearby cabinet.
- A plastic "recycling center" from a home-furnishing store: These units stack vertically for the organized separation of different materials

and are an efficient use of space for an important ecological purpose. ● A small bucket placed in the sink will save you from bending and reaching to dispose of every small handful of garbage. Use any plastic container, with holes punched in the bottom, to drain liquids. After you've prepared the meal, just dump the smaller bucket into the undersink pail.

REFRIGERATOR/FREEZER

If space allows, a side-by-side model is preferable. Less reaching is required in the freezer area, compared with a standard freezer or a chest freezer, which is even less accessible. An outside ice dispenser is a convenient feature for anyone with limited hand mobility.

DISHWASHER

The smart-aging kitchen design plan should consider two features in a dishwasher: the noise level, which disturbs some older adults more than others, and the amount of water used, which is an environmental consideration for all of us. Another important consideration is the size. Companies are now manufacturing dishwashers in several different heights to give consumers more flexibility in kitchen design. Dishwashers can be installed under countertops that have been lowered to a more convenient height; there are even compact units available that can be installed above the countertop, for those who prefer to avoid any bending at all.

● **JENN-AIR'S ULTIMATE QUIET SERIES:** An excellent choice if noise is a problem; the machine uses seven to ten gallons of water per cycle.
● **ASKO:** This compact unit can be installed at any height to reduce repetitive bending; it has a reasonably quiet motor and conserves water (5.3 gallons per cycle).

SINK

The sink's location largely determines the kitchen "traffic flow" or how much the cook must move around.

- A corner location is a good use of corner space that is otherwise difficult to use efficiently.
- Under a window is a pleasant spot for the sink. This location provides natural daylight as well as visual entertainment.
- Two sinks in a kitchen with multiple cooks is handy if room permits; their placement should be distant enough to prevent "traffic congestion."

Because the sink is essential in cooking, it must be installed at a height comfortable for those who frequently cook. The most effective way to assure this is by placing the sink in an adjustable-height countertop. To provide maximum flexibility, whereby a cook could actually sit at the sink, you should select a shallow sink with a drain in the rear. The use of flexible, plastic plumbing lines, available at most hardware stores, is preferable to rigid PVC pipes; these will give you the option of raising or lowering the sink with little effort at some point in the future. If you want to design the sink so that you can sit at it rather than stand, remember that pipes must be insulated, as well as the bottom of the sink.

- Depth: Sinks are ordinarily seven to eight inches deep, but shallow sinks of 5 to 6½ inches are made by American Standard, Elkay, and Kindred. If you're standing, you needn't reach as far, or lean forward as much, if you have a shallow sink. If you're seated, the shallow sink is less trouble to slide your legs underneath.
- Adjustable-height sinks: This sink is supported by cleats screwed to an adjacent cabinet or wall. The cleats can be lowered or raised. Motorized adjustment is also available in a unit designed by Accessible Designs. Any sink or countertop you select can be lowered from

twenty-eight inches and raised to forty inches with a simple switch; the motor is installed under the sink.

• Double sinks are also available in shallow models from American Standard and Elkay.

• A single-lever faucet is the best choice for all sinks because it can be manipulated without fine motor skills.

• A faucet with a long hose attached lets you fill pots on a nearby cooktop without heavy lifting.

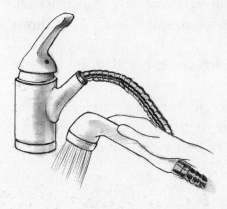

Kitchen sinks can be equipped with a hot-water dispenser, which is a great convenience, especially for individuals who frequently make soup or tea for themselves. The standard setting is usually 190 degrees Fahrenheit, though the temperature setting can be adjusted. CAUTION: If anyone using the kitchen has memory impairment, hot-water dispensers can be dangerous.

Lever faucet with pull-out hose.

INSTANT KITCHEN

All your appliances can be purchased in one stop by buying an already-assembled kitchen unit. This unit measures approximately 51 by 26 by 84 inches (length, depth, height), and it can be installed in an efficiency apartment or a home as a simple, small kitchen. The unit includes an electric or microwave oven, burners, refrigerator, sink, and storage cabinets. A nearby supply of hot and cold water and sufficient electricity is all that's required to make the unit functional.

WASHER AND DRYER

If space permits, it's convenient to have the washer and dryer in the kitchen. This allows a homemaker to complete several chores at once and to avoid walking long distances to an often cold and distant garage or basement to do laundry. Many new appliances are available that are well suited to a smart-aging home:

- **VENTLESS COMBINATION WASHER-DRYER:** Automatic conversion of condensate to water allows installation without any construction; moisture extracted from drying is converted to water and flushes down the drain.
- **STACKED WASHER-DRYER:** A good space saver, but ill-suited to use by anyone in a wheelchair.
- **PLATFORM FOR FRONTLOADERS:** To avoid bending with heavy wet clothes, consider a front-loading washer or dryer that is placed on a simple platform to make the door height easily accessible.

Work Surfaces and Storage Units

COUNTERTOPS

If you've ever written letters at a desk that was too high or have put together a jigsaw puzzle on a table designed for children, you and your back will remember the experience vividly. The height of any work surface is one of the single most important determinants in creating a physically comfortable space.

Standard base cabinets are 34½ inches tall, which includes a four-inch toe-kick space. The countertop material adds another 1½ inches, bringing the standard kitchen work surface to thirty-six inches. If you are particularly short or tall, remember that the ideal countertop height is typically six inches below your elbow, measured while you are standing. Adjustments can be made to customize the height of your work surface in the following ways:

- Have cabinets custom built to suit your preferred height.
- Order standard-built cabinets and remove the toe kick, reducing the height to thirty-two inches. Be sure cabinet doors can still swing open properly without dragging on the floor. Taller cooks can replace the four-inch toe-kick with a six- to eight-inch toekick, creating a thirty-eight- to forty-inch countertop height.
- Install an electrical adjustable countertop in at least one section of the work area. An area beside the sink, where there are no cabinets underneath, is an ideal spot. The surface can be used by children or by adults who prefer to work sitting down. A motorized unit from Accessible Designs can be used for adjusting countertops as easily as it is used for adjusting sink heights. The maximum countertop height with this motorized unit is forty inches; the minimum, twenty-eight inches. A countertop thirty inches high is generally well suited for the average adult when seated.

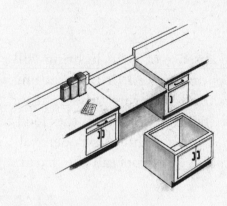

Removable base cabinet and adjustable-height countertop.

Remember, in designing a smart-aging kitchen, flexibility is crucial. Even if you now have no particular need for an adjustable-height countertop, it's wise to plan for contingencies. At least one section of base cabinet thirty-six inches wide should be designated for possible removal later; the floor surface beneath it should be finished, as should the sides of the adjacent cabinets. The countertop on this section of cabinetry should be screwed into the wall and not into the base cabinets in order to provide for easy removal later.

The use of all countertops in the kitchen is greatly enhanced by choosing the proper surface material. With today's choices, it is entirely possible to have the best of both aesthetics and practicality.

- Choose a matte finish to reduce glare. Light colors offer greater visual contrast with the food and utensils. Look for durable, even surface materials such as Corian or plastic laminate.
- Avoid materials such as tiles that create a visually pleasing effect but are not totally level.
- Except for stainless steel, most surfaces are not designed to withstand hot pots taken directly from the oven or the burner; to be sure that the countertop is not damaged, provide an array of trivets or metal grills on the counter to receive very hot pots or casseroles.
- Consider a laminate countertop with a no-drip edge; this one-eighth inch lip around all or part of the countertop will prevent your having to bend and clean spills from the floor.

No matter what surface material is used, the absence of good lighting will eliminate the value of any selection. Counters can be well lit by installing fluorescent bulbs under the hanging cabinets. Full-spectrum tube lighting best approximates daylight and shows the natural colors of the food, whereas "cool" fluorescence provide a harsh, bluish light. A wooden valance can be added on the front of the cabinet to conceal the fixture mounted below it.

STORAGE UNITS

No one has ever been heard to complain that their kitchen has too much storage space. A law must exist that says however much cabinet space is provided in the kitchen, a sufficient quantity of pots and other paraphernalia will generate to fill it. Still, much kitchen storage space is often useless, because it is difficult to reach. Smart-aging design is based on the premise that storage space must be easily reached, accessible for those with limited mobility, and aesthetically pleasing. Remember this organizational principle: Frequently used utensils should be within easy reach and close to the appliance or the area where they will be used.

- Cabinet height is a personal decision, based on the stature of the cook(s). Hang upper cabinets on commercial brackets to make height adjustments easy at a later date. The standard height is eighteen to twenty-four inches from the countertop, but consider twelve to fifteen inches instead, which makes the second shelf more accessible.
- Motorized cabinets are a luxurious alternative. The simple flick of a switch moves the cabinet up and down; a manual pull system is also available from Cabinetmate. It lowers a hanging cabinet to countertop level.
- Frameless cabinets provide more storage space for small kitchens.
- "Knife" hinges on the cabinets allow doors to be folded back flush (at 180 degrees), preventing awkward acrobatics in ducking open doors.
- Magnetic touch latches allow cabinet doors to be opened with minimal strength; with nonmagnetic latches, colorful C handles are the best choice because they are both easy to see when contrasted against light-colored cabinetry and easy to grasp.
- Doors can be removed from cabinetry altogether, making access much easier, especially for the frail or visually impaired. To prevent the buildup of grease in open cabinetry, make sure the fan in the range hood is connected to the outside, or install an inexpensive exhaust window fan to draw out cooking fumes that carry grease.
- Cabinets can be fitted with pullout shelves or wire baskets to avoid bending and reaching toward the back of the shelf; lazy Susans are useful on stationary shelves, in both upper and lower cabinets.
- A walk-in pantry, if space provides, is a handy alternative to cabinets hung around the perimeter of the kitchen. If a blank wall can be made to accommodate even six-inch-deep shelving between studs, reliance on higher wall cabinets for storage can be substantially re-

duced. Even a small closet can be converted to a pantry, with ten- to twelve-inch pull-out shelving hung on heavy-duty industrial tracks.

• Pots and pans that are used frequently should be hung on a wall or a rack near the range, not above it where they will collect grease. Racks can also be attached to the back of cabinet doors.

• Narrow, six- to eight-inch shelves can be installed under the upper cabinets for easy access to items used regularly.

• Shelf reorganization is often the most successful approach to creating more storage space. A dozen dinner plates and glasses need not be stored on the most accessible shelf if you only entertain once or twice a year.

• Divide your twelve-inch shelves horizontally with a five-inch high, free-standing wire shelf insert. It will double your storage space and eliminate piling too many dishes on top of one another.

• Drawer space can be reorganized to eliminate a hazardous accumulation of loose knives. Use a wall-mounted magnetic knife holder or a free-standing butcher-block holder.

Safety

FIRE SAFETY

Most house fires start in the kitchen. Because this room obviously presents more hazards, additional care must be taken to protect against the possibility of a kitchen fire. A smoke detector should be placed just outside the kitchen, away from ordinary cooking smoke, to avoid setting off the alarm unintentionally. Also, check the batteries regularly, or buy a smoke detector with lithium batteries that last for ten years. Another option is to buy hardwired appliances, but you will still need a backup battery smoke alarm in case of a power outage. In addition, take the following precautions:

• Place a fire extinguisher within easy reach near the kitchen, and be sure you know how to use it. An extinguisher does not put out fires simply by hanging in the corner. If you first need to find the directions, then read and understand them before using the equipment, chances are your kitchen fire will quickly burn out of control. Check the extinguisher periodically, according to the manufacturer's directions, to be sure it is in proper working order for any fire emergency.

• Hang pot holders, towels, and other flammable items away from the stove.

• Install a fire suppressant system directly into your existing range-hood cabinet above the stove or cooktop. Any fire on this surface will immediately release the fire extinguisher valve and simultaneously shut off the gas or electricity leading to the stove.

• Clean oven and range hood regularly to avoid grease buildup.

• Install automatic shutoff timer on electric stoves, to reduce the possibility of unattended or forgotten pots that might catch fire.

• Wear tight-fitting sleeves or use rubber bands around loose ones when cooking so that clothing does not catch fire on an open gas flame.

• Use an electric teakettle that shuts off automatically when the water boils or the kettle boils dry.

• Use a portable timer that can be taken with you to different rooms. Most kitchen fires start because the cook forgot about the food left on the stove when the phone rang in another room or because the cook became absorbed in something else in another part of the house.

• If you're a smoker, confine your smoking to one area of the house; furniture is the first material to be ignited in a smoking fire, so your smoker's chair should be covered in fire-resistant upholstery fabric. *Never smoke in bed.*

• Keep a metal can for the sole purpose of discarding used smoking material; more than 60 percent of fires started by smokers are due to abandoned or discarded cigarettes, matches, or tobacco that "were not quite out."

FLOOR SAFETY

Kitchen floors generally aren't carpeted and, therefore, can present a hazard if you spill food or water on them. It's important to choose a flooring material that is not slippery when wet. This property is measured by a standard called the coefficient of friction. Select a flooring that has a friction rating of more than 0.6. Also, be aware that

- Linoleum and vinyl floors are easier and less fatiguing to stand on for long periods than are hard tile surfaces. Specify flooring with a matte finish because a waxy finish on a shiny floor will be very slippery underfoot.
- Wood flooring is a beautiful, natural material and relatively easy to maintain. It is a hard surface, however, and can be very tiring to stand on for long intervals. If you do choose wood flooring, use a matte finish; it will be less slippery.
- Mottled color tones are best suited to hide dirt or skid marks from wheels.
- A vinyl mat is a useful addition in front of a sink or work area because it reduces fatigue and serves as a sturdy, nonslip carpet. It does, however, require caution since, not being flush with the floor, it will require a small step up and might be inappropriate for anyone with a shuffling gate or a walker.

LIGHTING AND
ELECTRICAL SAFETY

Proper lighting will make all surfaces, including the floor, more visible and, therefore, safer. There are two principal types of lighting: general lighting, referring to the overall illumination that comes from daylight or from overhead fixtures, and task-specific lighting. Both are important in the kitchen. Ceiling fixtures with multiple bulbs are a mixed blessing:

They light well, but frequent trips up and down a ladder to change bulbs are an invitation to an accident. Look for fixtures that accept long-lived, easy-to-change bulbs. An economic choice is surface-mounted fluorescent fixtures with white acrylic panels; use only full-spectrum or warm white bulbs; they should last for several years. In addition,

- Install full-spectrum or warm white fluorescent fixtures under the cabinets for task-specific lighting.
- Add lighting over the range and sink or other places where you work a lot.
- Install light switches and electrical outlets no higher than forty-eight inches from the floor.
- Control glare by applying polyester film over the windows, adding blinds inside, or hanging awnings outside.
- Install surface-mounted cable raceway at the back of the counter or under the cabinets to increase the number of electrical outlets available for small appliances at a minimum expense. Be sure that all outlets, especially those near water, have been changed to ground-fault-interrupt outlets to avoid the possibility of shock.
- Have your electrician relocate your fuse box or service panel to an accessible area in your kitchen or nearby hallway.
- If extension cords must be used, select only those with a built-in circuit breaker. Extension cords are rated by the thickness or the gauge of the wire used. Many cords are intended only for use with table lamps and present a fire hazard when used for kitchen appliances with a heavy electrical draw. Read the gauge of the wire on the extension cord tab to see whether it is adequate for the appliance you are using.
- Many older homes have a sixty-amp service panel, whereas the minimum used today is one hundred amps. Current safety codes demand separate circuits for appliances such as microwaves and refrigerators. If renovating your kitchen, ask your electrician about the need to upgrade the electrical power and whether worn-out insulation around the wiring should be replaced at the same time.

Smart-Aging Kitchen Gadgets and Ideas

1. Long-handled "reachers" make reaching lightweight items on high shelves manageable without a step stool.

2. A step stool with an extra-high rail to grab and nonskid steps is much safer than a ladder or a conventional step stool.

3. Color-contrasted cover plates for electric switches make it much easier to see wall switches.

4. Electric can opener or nonslip cloth called a "grip enhancer."

5. A rocking knife is much easier to use than an ordinary knife that puts more pressure on joints and requires more force.

6. Make a cutting board that can be used with one hand. Take an ordinary wooden cutting board and glue or nail two wooden strips to it for an "L" shape in the corner. This will prevent food from sliding off. Rub the wood with vegetable oil. Then drill two holes and insert two stainless-steel nails to hold food in place for peeling and slicing. Add suction cups on the bottom, or place on a nonslip mat.

Step stool with safety railing.

7. Nonslip mixing bowls that can be used with one hand.

8. Easy-to-use peeler such as "Good Grips." This peeler has a built-up handle and a swivel blade that requires minimal wrist movement.

9. Oven dial turner with an L-shaped handle and plastic prongs fits over any dial up to 1¼ inches.

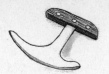

Rocker knife and cutting board for one-hand use.

10. Easy-pour container attachments.

11. Lazy Susans for use on all shelves where items in the back can't be seen or easily reached.

12. An adjustable-height dining tray/table with castors. This is a much safer and easier way to move food than carrying one hot plate at a time.

13. A foldup table to be used when sitting down to do light kitchen chores, such as chopping.

14. A cutting board that fits over a wheelchair.

15. Lightweight stainless-steel pot (in several sizes) from The Lighthouse Consumer Products Catalogue. The pots have self-locking lids with pre-drilled holes to empty hot water without burning yourself.

16. Lightweight pots with "stay cool" handles, or "cool handles" pot holders that slip over existing pots and pans.

17. Lightweight pot with easy-to-hold handles on both sides, available from the Enrichments catalog.

Pot with handles.

CHAPTER 8

The Smart-Aging Bathroom

A GLAMOROUS bathroom is to the nineties what the magnificently designed kitchen was to the eighties. No longer a purely utilitarian necessity, a new bathroom now accommodates luxurious features never dreamed of by architects or builders even ten years ago. But the real innovation in bathroom design is not always obvious to an untrained eye. New product concept and new recognition of an elder generation's special needs have convinced cutting-edge designers to include certain features that make the bathroom safe and useful for those with particular physical needs. Usually, these special features are so stylishly designed that they look like an integral part of the smart new bathroom, not merely a recognition of special requirements.

If you live in a multistory house without any complete bathroom facilities on the first floor, you should consider that what might not be an inconvenience for young, active adults could very well become a major problem in later years or even

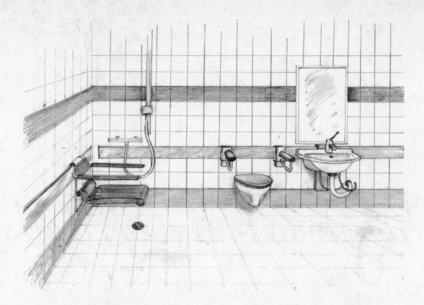

The Pressalit System by American Standard. The sink and the shower chair are mounted on a horizontal track; in a small space, where a caregiver may be required or a mobility aid needed, the units can be moved aside to provide additional space.

sooner, should a health catastrophe occur. Sweden now mandates that all new homes must have a full bathroom—one with toilet, sink, and either a tub or shower—on the first floor, and many of us with relatives who have been injured or friends who have aged, realize that often it is simply impossible to go up and down stairs several times a day. Sometimes, a downstairs closet can be enlarged and converted to a bathroom or a half bath—one with sink and toilet. You may find that you have more space than you think and you can add a shower by expanding into an adjacent room.

Many personal accidents in the home take place in the bathroom. This is not particularly surprising when you realize the acrobatics that are required to climb in and out of a bathtub and the potential for falling on a wet, slippery floor. Because bathrooms are expensive to renovate, given the requirement of specialty trades to complete plumbing and electrical changes, it behooves the homeowner to do it right the first time.

If you are in the fortunate position of building a new home or adding a new bath, the ideas that follow will enable you to create a functional, flexible bathroom that is adaptable to all ages and to most physical conditions. On the other hand, if you must renovate to accommodate the special needs of an older person or in anticipation of the possible frailties of older adults, study the second section on "Planning a Retrofit" (page 106). Significant changes can be made without spending a small fortune!

For example, just the addition of grab bars and night-lights will immeasurably increase safety in the bathroom.

Planning a New Bath

In older homes, bathrooms were built using the smallest amount of space possible. A five-by-seven-foot bathroom was typical, with limited storage, no seating other than the toilet, poor ventilation, and inadequate light. Today's smart-aging bathroom is a larger space, with at least five feet of turning space for a wheelchair or walker, and a choice of appliances and design features that accommodates the physical changes that usually accompany aging.

DOORS: Pocket doors are an excellent way to save space that may be at a premium, but if conventional doors are used in the bathroom, they should be hinged to open out toward the hall, rather than into the bathroom. Should anyone fall against the door while using the bathroom, this precaution ensures that those trying to help are not barred from entering. Pocket doors should be on high-quality ball-bearing tracks, to make them easy to operate. All door openings must be at least thirty-two to thirty-six inches to accommodate mobility aids.

GRAB BARS: Use of any facilities in the bathroom requires physical exertion, and any amount of physical effort is made easier by grab bars. No longer are grab bars available only in institutional-looking stainless steel. They are now found in many attractive decorator colors such as cranberry red, canary yellow, and pine green. Horizontal grab bars can be attached directly to the toilet to facilitate pushing off, as well as inside the tub area, to make stepping in and out much safer. A wall unit that can be swung up out of the way is also available; it is useful for people with walkers where stationary grab bars on a toilet might interfere. All grab bars should be made of nonslip material. High-quality nylon with a "locking grip" is one such material.

For new construction, there are two ways to properly install wall-mounted grab bars. The inside of the wall can be prepared during construction by installing either a plywood sheet that covers the entire wall (this way you can place the grab bars in any location) or by installing two-by-six-inch boards mounted horizontally so that the top of the boards is three feet from the floor.

A grab bar screwed into sheet rock is insufficient to support the weight of an adult, and that can be even more dangerous than not having any grab bars at all. The proper height of the bar depends on the person, but on average, thirty-three to thirty-six inches from the floor is appropriate. Many people find that a grab bar hung vertically at the edge of the shower or tub is helpful in maintaining balance when stepping in or out.

SINKS AND FAUCETS: Mount the sink wherever it is most comfortable for the person using it. The most common height is thirty-two inches, which requires considerable bending, particularly for a tall person, who would find a thirty-four- to thirty-eight-inch height more appropriate. Be sure to use flexible piping that will allow a height adjustment in either direction. To minimize reaching, the sink should be set into the vanity or countertop as close as possible to the front edge. A built-in "adaptable" vanity underneath, with removable doors and cabinet bottom will meet your current storage needs while providing the option of a sink height appropriate for sitting if this choice is later desired.

A more versatile height-adjustment mechanism is available with Pressalit, a motorized pump unit that moves the sink both horizontally and vertically. This is an excellent choice for those who want to move the sink instantly where, for example, there are several people in a household with different height requirements. Any sink that is used in a seated position must have the pipes underneath covered with insulation or a protective panel installed in front of them to prevent burning. For sitting at a sink, the proper height of the vanity is approximately thirty-two to thirty-four inches; leg room of twenty-seven to twenty-nine inches must be available under the sink. Storage capacity can then be shifted to drawers on either side of the vanity, space permitting. Two people with different needs may find it easier to install a second sink at a different height rather than to rely on one that is adjustable. If the additional sink is a wall-mounted unit, it should be installed with extra-strength brackets or with extra bracing, because it can pull loose if someone leans on it.

For ease of operation, install a single-lever faucet. This model offers both temperature and volume control in one unit, and is operable with one hand. Most lever faucets are available in chrome and brass, and can be ordered with an almond or white finish.

TOILETS: Newer toilets are wall mounted rather than floor mounted and, therefore, make cleaning the bathroom floor much easier. They also require less water, making them an ecologically better choice, but they are relatively expensive to install. A good choice for wheelchair users is a toilet with an elongated seat shape that is eighteen inches from the floor. The height makes transferring from a wheelchair fairly simple. It also makes getting off the toilet easier, particularly for those with arthritic knees, though the height can sometimes interfere with the process of elimination. You can also buy a plastic seat that adds two to five inches in height and can be easily attached to the existing toilet seat. If possible, locate the toilet with open space on either side, not in a corner, so it can be approached from either side if a wheelchair or walker is being used.

BATHTUB: If space permits, a bathtub is a nice inclusion, but a shower may be more practical. Certainly if a bathtub is added and an older adult is the primary user, it would be wise to consider a bathtub with an easy-access door. No climbing over high sides and onto slippery surfaces is necessary with these tubs; you open a door and step in. Think about including a quick-fill deck-mounted faucet that fills at twice the rate of an ordinary faucet, and a ceiling-mounted heat lamp for warmth for before and after bathing.

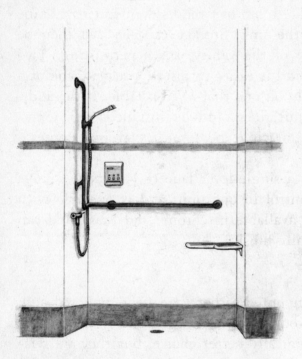

A barrier-free shower with a fold-down seat.

SHOWERS: New shower design often incorporates a shower spa in which the shower is an integral part of the room. The floor is sloped to carry away gray water, and only a curtain separates the showering area from the rest of the bathroom. This arrangement eliminates the cost of buying a shower unit and also does away with a frequent tripping hazard in the bathroom, namely, the two-inch lip of a conventional shower unit.

If you prefer a traditional shower, buy the largest unit that will fit the designated space. Standard units as small as thirty-six by thirty-six inches are available, but a sixty by sixty-inch unit is more comfortable for the bather and is suited to assisted showering if a frail or a recuperating patient needs help. Essential design elements in the smart-aging shower include a fold-down seat, a handheld shower unit, an antiscald shower head control, and grab bars on both walls adjacent to that on which the shower seat is affixed. Many manufacturers sell shower units complete with all these fixtures included. A low-cost alternative to a fold-down seat is a free-standing plastic stool with perforations in the seat for water drainage and nonskid rubber feet. Shower curtains are preferable to shower doors, which are sometimes difficult to slide.

VENTILATION, LIGHTING, AND ELECTRICAL SYSTEMS: Include a ceiling-mounted heat lamp if you are designing a new smart-aging bathroom; it's an inexpensive luxury for all ages and especially important for older people. Thermoregulators in the body do not work as well as we age, and after a shower or bath, a chill can come on quickly. A ceiling vent and fan should also be included but on a separate switch from the overhead light; otherwise, the continual fan noise becomes bothersome. Newly designed exhaust products, including the Broan "solitaire-ultra," create barely noticeable noise. A fan is important because good ventilation and air movement make the floors less slippery. A recessed vapor-proof light fixture should be installed in the shower area, in addition to glare-free incandescent lighting over the mirror. Be sure your electrician is instructed to have all outlets "ground-fault interrupted" so the risk of shock is completely eliminated. And as a last safety precaution, it is wise to include an emergency call button or a telephone mounted near the bathtub.

LAUNDRY FACILITIES: Many people find that if space permits, the most logical place for the laundry is in the bathroom. Generally, it is near the bedroom, where soiled clothes and bed linens accumulate, and the obvious place where used towels are thrown. Compact washer-dryer combinations can be bought that let you do small loads of wash easily even if you have a larger washer and dryer on another floor of the house.

FLOORS: Bathroom floors must be chosen not only for their beauty, but also for their safety, meaning that the flooring must be a nonslip surface. The coefficient of friction (COF) is the measure of how "nonslip" a floor material really is. The higher the number on this industry-wide scale, the more slip-resistant the surface. Look for a flooring product with a COF of 0.6 or higher. Because institutional buyers demand it, virtually all commercial products include this rating, whereas some of the products oriented to residential buyers don't. The availability of a COF rating is one reason to consider buying a commercial, or industrial, product: so much more testing has typically been conducted on this class of products than on the more fashion-oriented consumer lines. The other reason, of course, is that commercial products today have largely lost their "institutional look" and are often as attractive as anything else found in designer showrooms.

Apart from choosing a floor with a high coefficient of friction, look for vinyl or other relatively soft materials that are waterproof rather than ceramic tiles that are usually cold and much harder. If you really must have ceramic tiles, choose the smallest ones possible; they are safer than large tiles. Be sure, too, that they are nonglazed and nonslip. A line of vinyl sheet flooring manufactured by Altro Flooring is so resistant to moisture that it can actually be used throughout the bathroom, even one that includes a spa shower. But if the flooring has any seams, be sure the installer heat-welds the seams, so water cannot leak underneath. For those who prefer carpeting for its warmth and softness underfoot, mildew-proof carpeting is available from some manufacturers. Though regular carpeting is not well suited to a bathroom, specialized carpeting offers some protection against severe injury if a fall occurs. It also eliminates the need for an additional bath mat, which can be hazardous underfoot.

Planning a Retrofit

If you're not planning to add a new bathroom, it is still possible to make smart-aging changes or renovations to your existing bathroom, many of which can alleviate serious problems without major expense. Consider the following items to see which ideas can be incorporated into your present home.

SHOWER INSTALLATION: If your downstairs has a "half bath," adding a shower could make a major difference to someone who has difficulty climbing stairs and wants to consolidate living on the first floor. Prefab units in many sizes are available, but a thirty-nine by sixty-inch unit, Warm Rain, manufactured by the company Great Lakes Plastic, is the smallest recommended. The larger the shower size, the easier it is for a caregiver to help if it is ever required. A large shower unit also helps keep the water inside the shower stall. Be sure to choose a shower unit sized to fit through your existing doors or to buy a "break-down unit" that can be reassembled on site. Some units come equipped with fold-up seats, grab bars, and an antiscald shower control, all of which are highly desirable features. Or if arthritis or other problems make climbing over the bathtub difficult, think about removing the existing tub and replacing it with a shower that fits the same space.

HANDHELD SHOWER UNIT: These units usually come equipped with a large handle and five-foot-long hose for easy holding, and are ideal for those who prefer to shower while seated. Depending on the model, the hose is attached to the bathtub spout or to the original shower head arm. For hands-free showering, a two-to-three-foot vertical track lets the bather easily move the shower head up or down. An added convenience is a shower head with the water controls located in the head itself; this means you need never reach far to adjust the flow. If you have sensitive skin, you will appreciate the soft, aerated spray option.

ANTISCALD SHOWER CONTROL: Water temperature should be set no higher than 120 degrees Fahrenheit, but in a house with older plumbing, a toilet flushed in one bathroom may cause the water temperature in the shower in another bathroom to become scalding. An antiscald shower control contains a sensor that automatically turns off the water when it reaches a set temperature. If you are buying new faucets and shower heads, you might find that this feature is often incorporated. And if you are mounting new faucets and shower heads, place the controls near the entry point of the shower, not in the middle.

BATHROOM TELEPHONE: A permanent or portable phone is essential so that anyone who falls or is unwell in the bathroom can call for help.

SEATING SPACE: If possible, include a sturdy chair with arms to make rising easy.

GRAB BARS: Add grab bars to the existing shower and bath walls. They can be mounted directly on the bathroom wall, installed with long screws into wall studs. Your handyman can locate the studs with a good stud-finding tool. If locating the studs is a problem, as can be the case with ceramic walls, surface mount the grab bar on a solid wood board sized slightly larger than the grab bar. Slope the top of the board to allow water runoff, apply a waterproof finish, and securely attach to the wall, caulking around the edges. Grab bars can also be installed on the wall next to the toilet or directly on the toilet, if required.

GLARE-FREE LIGHTING: Add glare-free lighting over the medicine cabinet.

SENSOR-ACTIVATED FAUCETS: These faucets are helpful if arthritis or other health problems make manipulation of faucets difficult. Lever faucets with antiscald protection are another good choice. Install the faucet on the side of the sink for easy access.

The Elder Bathroom

If designing a new bathroom or retrofitting an older one is a bigger task than you want to take on, you soon will be able to turn over the design

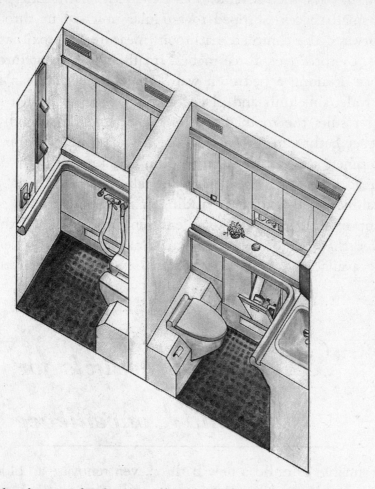

Safety features of Robert Graeff's elder bathroom include wrap-around grab bars along the countertop and shower walls and lighting at floor level for nighttime use.

problem to architects who have carefully thought through all the issues associated with the special needs of older adults. This is not a particularly low-cost solution, but it will be an instant fix if you're interested in adding a safe, functional bathroom right away.

Robert Graeff, an architect at Virginia Polytechnic Institute and State

University, has designed several models of "elder bathrooms" that are well suited to small spaces. Shipped in modular units to fit through existing home doorways, the complete bathroom measures approximately ten feet, ten inches, by three feet, three inches, small enough to fit into an existing closet space or along a bedroom wall. The shower unit can be separated from the toilet/sink unit and placed along a separate wall if this arrangement better suits the room. Some of the other elder-friendly features of this compact bathroom retrofit include lights along the nonslip flooring, bottom cabinets with upward-protruding containers so you don't need to bend to reach the lowest spaces of the cabinet, magnifying glass on the edge of cabinet shelves for easy reading of medicine bottles, cabinet doors that roll up or slide sideways, excellent ventilation, and all the features in the shower that are designed for maximum safety. The entire system should be available by 1997, as well as several variations the following year.

Bathroom Products for Safety and Convenience

If you are unable to build a new bath or even renovate an older one, there are products on the market that can be instantly installed, making bathroom use much safer and easier for an elder. Many of them are quite inexpensive.

- **A BATHTUB TRANSFER BENCH:** This four-legged bench is placed so that two legs are in the tub and two stay outside on the bathroom floor, all steadily secured by suction cups. You slide across the bench and are able to slip the curtain through an opening in the bench, so you can effectively shower while seated. The device is not suited to old-fashioned ball and claw tubs.

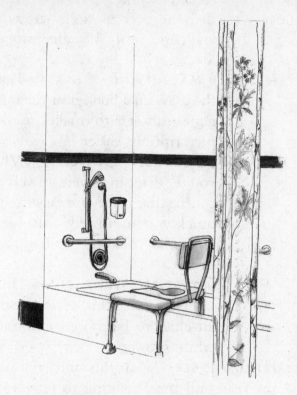

Getting in and out of the bathtub is easier and safer with a transfer chair that you slide across. Other features include a handheld shower hose, sensor soap dispenser, and grab bars. The location of grab bars should be individually chosen, depending on where a hand support is needed.

● **BATHTUB GRAB BARS:** These attach to the rim of the bathtub rather than to the wall and are easy to hold on to when getting in or out of the tub. They attach without tools and are tension adjustable.

● **TUB SWIVEL CHAIR:** This device slides from side to side, locking into place for safety. It does not lower into the bathtub but allows the bather to create a shower effect while seated in the bathtub. A handheld shower device should be fitted to the bathtub spout.

● **BATH LIFTS:** Units are either hydraulically or battery operated and vary in cost. They move the bather from the rim of the tub to the bottom of the tub and are ideal in assisting those who need routine, therapeutic soaking in a hot tub.

● **EASY-REACH STORAGE UNITS:** Large medicine cabinets are available and should be mounted at a height accessible to the user. Mounting a medicine cabinet on the side of the sink reduces bending and reaching for either a seated or standing user. Vanities with features such as open shelves at the corners, pullout trays at the base, or shelving on one side, make the contents more easily reachable. Poles with at-

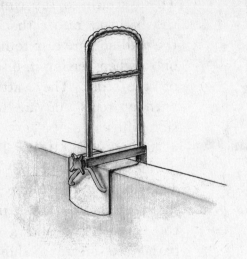

Bathtub grab bar.

tached storage trays or open shelving over the toilet are other low-cost, easily installed storage ideas.

● **MAGNIFYING GLASS:** Hang the glass on a hook near the medicine cabinet to make reading prescriptions easier.

● **COLORED TOWELS:** When you're dripping wet, towels in contrasting colors are easier to see quickly than towels that blend with the color of the bathroom wall.

● **RUST-RESISTANT CHAIR:** In a larger shower, this device enables an elder to be more comfortable while showering.

● **SHOWER WALL SENSOR SOAP DISPENSER:** With this unit, you need not worry about dropping the soap and then bending to retrieve it, because soap is automatically dispensed when your hand is placed under the unit.

CHAPTER 9

Designing for Specific Physical Conditions

ALTHOUGH AGING does not always bring on disease, the body declines and certain physical limitations are inevitable. The National Institute on Disability and Rehabilitation has found that arthritis is the most common chronic condition restricting ordinary daily activities for people over sixty-five years old. The second and third most frequent conditions are heart disease and vision loss. Yet the impact of these conditions can be lessened by a variety of products, techniques, and concepts that compensate for restricted mobility, frailty, and low vision—in other words, by smart-aging design.

If you are coping with a debilitating medical condition or are caring for one who is, this chapter will help you identify design solutions for the functional limitations that many common medical conditions create. My objective here is not to assess the impact of specific diseases, but to identify the practical issues and the specific, day-to-day problems presented to those with health limitations. Just as medical practitioners are finding new medications and cures for disease, designers are inventing and improving household products that contribute to a comfortable, residential environment. Many of these products are listed in the "Resource Guide" at the end of the book.

Mobility Limitations

There are an infinite number of medical conditions where the cumulative impact results in generally lessened mobility, anything from minor arthritis that makes stair climbing difficult, to the more severe impact of a stroke. Mobility limitations may vary dramatically, but depending on one's personality, any capacity that is diminished creates a feeling of dependency and even depression. Self-help products and attention to proper design can make the home safer and provide its occupant with a more supportive environment.

Oftentimes, there are combinations of physical problems that manifest themselves in an inability to move well or to move certain parts of the body easily. Arthritis can cause reduced hand strength for some people, stiff knees for others, and sometimes just a limited ability to reach or to bend. In fact, any illness can sometimes be so enervating that a wheelchair is required, whether or not the actual symptoms represent mobility problems.

If you're rethinking the design features of your house, be it a new home or the renovation of an existing one, it is sensible to anticipate that your symptoms may become more pronounced in later years. The following list is for those with medical conditions that have resulted in limited hand strength or relatively minor mobility problems. Illnesses such as Parkinson's disease generally result in more serious movement limitations; greater attention to products and residential design can accommodate even severely restricted mobility. A second list is provided for this type of condition. If you want to accommodate the needs of a wheelchair user, a third section details many features that each room must incorporate to create a comfortable living environment. These lists are not mutually exclusive. You may be motivated to incorporate only those products or ideas that are required for a current condition, but to avoid the burden of multiple renovations, it is wise to consider the symptomatic progression of the disease and your future needs.

PRODUCTS AND IDEAS FOR THOSE WITH MINOR MOBILITY OR MOVEMENT RESTRICTIONS

Living Areas

- Replace or convert round doorknobs to lever-action closures.
- Use "touch-turn-on" controls for lamps, which can turn on lamps by touching rather than by turning a switch.
- Use "rocker" wall switches rather than toggle switches.

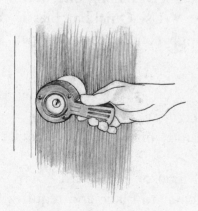

Lever adapter for doorknobs.

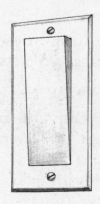

Rocker wall switch.

- Buy a headset rather than a handheld telephone unit.
- Install blinds with easy-to-use controls; they require less strength than pullcords.
- Use a telephone with large push-buttons.

Kitchen

STORAGE

- Loop a strap on the refrigerator/freezer door; it requires less strength to open. Also, placing heavy tape on lower door gasket makes the door open easily.
- Change small knobs on drawers and cabinets to large C handles, and fit round-knob water faucets with large-handled adapters.
- Put lazy Susans in refrigerator and storage cabinets.

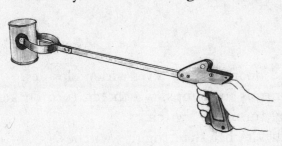

Long-handled "reacher."

- Add narrow shelves below upper cabinets for easier access and less reaching.
- Get a long-handled "reacher" for items on low or high shelves.
- Add shallow pantry shelves along one wall.
- Use Quickbox plastic containers for small items; these see-through containers snap open and close with light-handed pressure.

MEAL PREPARATION

- Electric can opener with grip enhancer
- Pot lid adapter to convert small knobs on top of lids to larger handles
- Cutting board with spikes that hold food on the board
- "Rocker" knives (handle is perpendicular to blade and requires less force for cutting)

- Mounted "jar opener" under cabinet
- Electric peeler or Good Grips ergonomic peeler
- Faucet hose, for filling pots directly from sink when they are already on stove top
- Lightweight pans with built-up handles on both sides

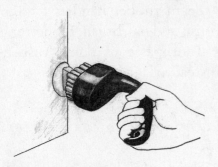

Knob turner.

Faucet turner.

- Large-handled "knob turner" for oven controls
- Lever faucets instead of turning knobs, or lever faucet adapter
- Dish brush with suction-cup base.

FOR EATING

Attractive, elder-friendly place setting includes easy-grip utensils, large-handled teacup, and a "scoop" dish.

- Round "scoop" dish, instead of flat plates
- Eating utensils with built-up handles, or add tubular foam rubber to the handles of utensils
- "Thumbs-up" drinking cup with large handles and thumb rests—cup can be raised without wrist motion
- "Rocker" knives, instead of ordinary table knives

Bathroom

Easy-grip rubber tubes can be placed over existing handles.

- Automatic infrared soap dispenser
- Foam rubber handles for toothbrush and hairbrush, for better grip
- Toothpaste in pump dispenser, instead of a squeeze tube

Bedroom and Closet

- Shoes and clothing with Velcro closures
- Dressing aids, including zipper and button pull, and a long-handled shoehorn
- Remote control unit with large numbers for draperies, blinds, lighting, stereo, and TV

PRODUCTS AND IDEAS FOR MORE SERIOUS RESTRICTIONS IN MOVEMENT OR MOBILITY

Some elders find they prefer to use mobility aids such as walkers, canes, or wheelchairs for only part of the day or for certain activities, and do without the aids at other times. Also, there are days that they may feel the need to use a cane but on other days feel as if they could walk a mile. Therefore, a residence should be designed to incorporate a mobility aid "just in case." In addition, some people have experienced an illness or accident that creates severe limitations. There are a number of products and design ideas that can be helpful.

Indoor and Outdoor Living Areas

- Remove all area rugs or tape them securely in place; on stairs, use nonslip treads and short-nap carpet. Or leave wood floors bare.
- Mount a cane holder (a clip with an adhesive back) next to the front door, in the bedroom, and in the living room, so the cane is never left on the floor.
- Install handrails on both sides of stairs or hallways.
- Install an electric chair or elevator in a two-story house, or consolidate living on one floor.
- Remove all door sills.
- Eliminate rocking chairs that might be used as a support when someone is standing or walking past; they tip easily and can be dangerous.
- Place vertical handles (grabbers) on inside of doorways that can be used for support when necessary.
- Outdoor walkways should be an even surface; no cracks, flagstone, or uneven tiles.
- Add outdoor benches and chairs in the garden or on the porch.
- If upper-body strength is very modest or restricted, consider a page-turning device from Touch Turner that will enable you to turn pages of a book or magazine by puffing into a straw.

Kitchen

FOOD PREPARATION

- Mixing bowl with suction cups
- Stay-put self-contained grater
- Teakettle tipper, a stationary wire holder that allows you to tip the kettle using very little body force
- Chair or stool for cook, and one counter section lowered to convenient height for a seated cook

Flooring with doorsill removed.

Chair lift.

- Forty-eight- to sixty-inch turning radius in center of kitchen to accommodate a walker
- Sink depth of 5 to 6½ inches—a shallow sink requires less bending
- Upper cabinets hung twelve inches from countertop rather than from the conventional eighteen to twenty-four inches above counter
- Base cabinet with sliding drawers, or cabinets with sliding shelves (in upper and lower cabinets)
- A cooktop with controls that are in the front of the unit for easier reaching, and a separate oven set in at a convenient height
- Cushioned, nonslip floor
- Railing on edge of countertop; a convenient hand grip for those with balance problems

EATING

- Plates with an inner lip that impedes spillage; plates with suction cups that stay firmly affixed to the table if tremors are a problem

- Single unit knife/fork that can be used with either hand to cut food into bite-sized pieces and bring them to your mouth
- Weighted spoons that help avoid spillage for people with tremors
- Weighted metal "arm" to assist those with tremors
- Two-handled mugs with spillproof tops
- Cups with long straws
- Pushcart for transporting food from kitchen to table, or a basket for the walker
- A battery-operated machine, The Windsor Feeder, that enables people to eat at their own rate without any arm effort; one touch of a switch raises an adjustable utensil and a second touch returns the device to the plate.

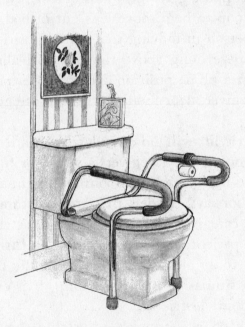

Adjustable-height grab bars fasten directly to the toilet, providing support for sitting down or standing up. An attachable paper-roll holder eliminates twisting and bending.

Bathroom

- Bathtub with doors, or wheel-in shower with handheld shower unit
- Bath seat that automatically lowers the bather into the tub
- Rubber suction mat in tub
- Grab bars at toilet and in shower/bath
- Antimold carpeting or nonslip resilient flooring
- Infrared automatic soap dispenser
- Large-handled electric toothbrush
- Handheld flosser that requires only one hand to floss

Bedroom

- Store canes or crutches in a container such as an umbrella stand that is accessible but safely out of the way, perhaps in a corner of the room.
- Install night-lights in hallways, near the top and bottom of stairs, and in bathrooms; if a night-light is placed in the bedroom, get one that is sensor activated, so it will not disturb sleep. Automatic ones come on at dusk and turn off at dawn.
- Eliminate all area rugs.
- Add a bed handle or rail for support getting in and out of bed.
- Use a "leg-lifter" strap with loop to help move legs out of bed.
- Buy an electric bed to aid a person in moving to a seated position.
- Install a trapeze grasp. A trapeze hung above the bed will allow patients to raise themselves from a prone position and to move more easily with less reliance on a caregiver; floor-mounted models are generally safer than others.
- Install a personal lift. An electric lift will aid considerably in lifting a heavy patient or even a light one if the caregiver is slight or frail. These lifts should be portable for use in both bedroom and bath, and narrow enough to fit through doorways. Models that are structurally sound and less difficult for the caregiver are those with a seat that tucks under the buttocks of the patient, requiring little or no lifting by the caregiver. An alternative to an electric lift is a hydraulic one that uses a pumping mechanism similar to a bicycle pump. It is easy to use and is less expensive than an electric lift.
- Install bifold or sliding doors on closets with adjustable shelves inside the closet.

PRODUCTS AND IDEAS FOR
WHEELCHAIRS USERS

Some permanent disabilities result in constant wheelchair use, and home design in such cases must accommodate the needs of an individual who is always seated. Elders, though, often use wheelchairs only at certain times during the day or when recuperating, and it is not as easy to think through design requirements when use of a wheelchair is sporadic, infrequent, or anticipatory. A five-foot turning radius is the most essential consideration, especially in the bathroom and kitchen, where spaces generally are tighter. Passing through doorways and negotiating stairs are also major problems. Remember that not only necessities such as light switches and medicine cabinets must be lowered, but also bending and reaching from a seated position can be particularly strenuous. Review the activities that are required repeatedly in the home, and design solutions that minimize physical exertion.

Indoor and Outdoor Living Areas

- Clear an unobstructed three- to four-foot pathway in every room and hallway.
- Place light switches thirty-six to thirty-eight inches from the floor, or adapt higher switches to this height with an "extender."
- Place electrical outlets eighteen to twenty-four inches from floor and thermostatic controls forty-four to forty-eight inches from floor.
- Install crank adapter for double-hung or sliding windows.
- Build a ramp to the outside (see chapter 5, pages 51 and 52–53, for details on construction).
- Add a second door handle, placed in the center of the door; it is easier for a wheelchair user to reach.
- All doorways with doors must have eighteen to twenty-four inches of space on the side where the door swings away from the chair, and

twenty-four inches of clear space where it pulls toward the chair. Install an automatic door opener if landing is smaller than this.

• Remove all doorsills that are more than one-quarter inch high.

Kitchen

• Eight-inch toe kick on cabinets, to accommodate the wheelchair footrest

• Side-by-side refrigerator/freezer, to provide easier access to a range of items in the unit; usually comes with smaller doors

• Angled mirror above cooktop or stove, to allow seated cook to see into pots on back burner of cooktop

• Pullout cutting boards

• Base cabinets with pullout drawers on full extension gliders; the sides of drawers should be cut low so the entire contents of the drawer are visible when fully extended.

• All countertop heights at a maximum of thirty-two inches from floor

• Kneehole space of thirty to thirty-six inches beneath cooktop, beside the oven, and under the sink

• Aisles of no less than forty-two inches

• Upper cabinets with slide-out shelves hung no more than twelve inches above countertop

• A clear space in front of appliances of at least thirty inches by forty-eight inches; this allows an approach from either the front or the side.

• A cooktop with controls that are in front of the unit for easier reaching and a separate oven set in at a convenient height

• If kitchen renovation is not a viable option, consider setting up a "minikitchen" with a thirty-inch-high table, a microwave, perhaps a hotplate, and a limited number of easily accessible tools for meal preparation.

Bathroom

- Adjustable sink height or one at thirty inches with no vanity below
- Hang a tilted mirror over the sink and the medicine cabinet on the side wall, thirty-four to thirty-eight inches from the floor.
- Grab bars at toilet and in shower/bath
- Wheel-in shower with handheld shower unit, transfer bench in bathtub, or hydraulic lift to move person from chair to bathing area

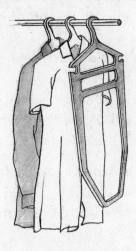

Bedroom

- Shallow closets with bifold doors and bars hung approximately forty-four inches from the floor
- Special 35½-inch-long Fitz closet hangers that are easy to reach from a seated position
- Bed height no more than eighteen inches from the floor, making transfer to the chair much simpler
- Electric carousel for clothing

The extra-long
Fitz hanger

SPECIALIZED MOBILITY AIDS

There is a wide variety of mobility aids, such as canes, walkers, wheelchairs, or scooters. Even within each of these product groups, there are variations in quality, design, and suitability for each buyer. Ask for advice from a physical or occupational therapist before making a purchase. A few general guidelines and product ideas follow.

CANES: Canes should be the proper size for your height and weight, and should always be used on the stronger side of your body. A four-pronged cane is ideal when balance problems are prevalent; a single-point cane is suited to a more precise, one-sided weakness. You might want to pick out one in a colorful metal or a polished wood grain. Raisin' Cane, a small company in Massachusetts, offers a line of canes that inspires many purchases for fashion, not medical purposes. Their canes are hand-painted or marbleized by talented artists, studded with crystals, or wrapped in ribbons and designer fabrics. All canes need a rubber cup at the bottom to prevent slipping.

- If you are out in cold weather, buy a protective cane tip for icy surfaces
- Attach a cane holder to the cane; it will let you rest it on a table surface, and it won't fall to the floor, where it can become a tripping hazard.

WALKERS: Walkers are available with wheels, and often, they're easier to use than ones that need to be picked up with every step. The rolling speed can be adjusted for almost any pace, allowing for a natural gait.

- Specialized U-Step Walker Stabilizer walkers are ideally suited for those with Parkinson's. They are easier to turn, and the rolling speed is adjustable.
- Many walkers come with adjustable seats and have weight-sensitive wheels that lock into place for safety when pressure is applied.

Clip-on holder. Cane designed by Raisin' Cane.

WHEELCHAIRS: One size does *not* fit all, and much like a pair of shoes, the wheelchair should be the proper size for the individual using it. A standard sling-back/sling-seat chair is generally not very comfortable for long pe-

The Rock 'N' Go wheelchair by Homecrest Healthcare.

riods, but for greater comfort, seating systems are available that adapt a standard chair.

- Jay Medical makes a back and seat system called Jay Care, which fits a standard chair, supports the pelvis, relieves pressure on the spine, and has a soft, comfortable fabric.
- Lightweight chairs, (currently *not* reimbursed by Medicare) weigh twenty to thirty pounds less than a standard chair and are easier to maneuver. Polymer tires are best suited to indoor use; pneumatic tires, best suited to outdoor.

- Homecrest Healthcare manufactures a new generation of wheelchairs made especially for seniors. The Rock 'N' Go model has large wheels in front for easy handling, a rocking motion to assist circulation, and a semireclining position for short naps. There is also a choice of fabrics for the chair.
- WayMaker by Pathfinder Enterprises Inc. is a standard-sized chair that, with a lever beneath the chair, can be narrowed from twenty-six inches to nineteen inches to pass through tight spaces. Because both hydraulic and mechanical pressure are used to move the chair forward or backward, it requires very little hand force to operate.

POWERED SCOOTERS: Many elders prefer scooters to other mobility aids because of the public's reaction to them. A senior speeding about on a scooter looks racy; one with a wheelchair may strike some people as simply "old." Choose a scooter that is easy to mount, one with good lumbar support, rear-wheel drive, and a 24-volt system for added power.

General Frailty

General frailty is technically defined as impairment of the physical abilities one needs to live independently; practically speaking, it is the cumulative effect of many minor impairments—in muscle strength, in posture and balance, in gait, and in bone mass. One cause of frailty is cardiovascular disease, but there are others as well. In and of itself, frailty may not be the primary problem. Frailty frequently causes falls and injury, often a hip fracture, which may not heal well. In designing a home for someone who is frail, you should recognize the frequent symptoms of frailty. Hypothermia (perpetually lowered body temperature) and hyperthermia (the general term used to describe a variety of heat-related illnesses) are both correlated with frailty, as is the tendency to bruise easily.

The onset of frailty and its accompanying loss of strength can be delayed considerably by exercise, which results in improved strength, coordination, and balance for even ninety-year-olds. Studies by the National Institute on Aging indicate that a proper exercise routine, combined with other measures, can reduce falls by at least 30 percent. In addition to exercise, there are several environmental changes and self-care products that help prevent accidents and increase mobility and activity in daily life, even for someone with significant functional limitations.

The second approach to delaying the onset of frailty is to make preventive environmental changes in your home. These modifications should serve two purposes: the prevention of falls, and energy conservation. Often, a fall leads to a serious downward spiral for an elderly patient, since a weakened immune system leads to longer recovery times and greater exposure to infection in hospital. Designing a home that will reduce the chances of a fall is the best protection a frail elder can buy. Second, a well-organized room can be critical in conserving limited energy. Frailty means that any physical exertion can be exhausting—even moving repeatedly from the stove to the refrigerator during meal preparation—so you must design spaces that reduce unnecessary physical effort. For cardiac patients, a well-organized room can be a life-saver.

Indoor and Outdoor Living Areas

- Add handrails on both sides of any stairs, or along one wall in the hallways.
- Select a four-wheeled walker with a seat rest.
- Attach plastic guards to edges of all furniture to prevent bruising.
- Be certain there is adequate lighting and an absence of clutter throughout the house.
- Weatherize exterior doors and windows, and use storm windows if appropriate; loss of heat in the house aggravates a hypothermic condition.
- Wear a waterproof emergency call pendant at all times.
- Select chairs that have a medium-firm seat, adequate cushioning to avoid bruising, and good lumbar support. The arms of the chair should extend past the seat itself. Inadequate chairs can be improved with attachable orthopedic seat and back.
- Remove all area carpets or rugs that might present a tripping hazard.
- Consolidate living activities on one floor to preserve strength.

Kitchen

- Simplify work areas and the entire room as much as possible; consolidate appliances in one area to cut down constant moving about; organize individual tasks such as washing or chopping, so they are all done at once.
- Keep often-used items on the countertop, on narrow shelves under the cabinets, or in drawers under the countertop, so that bending and reaching are unnecessary.

Smart-aging kitchen design includes seating for mealtime preparation and easy-to-reach storage.

- Keep nutritious frozen meals stocked in freezer, for times when energy flags.
- Consider ordering from Meals on Wheels, an organization, not a charity, whose meals are priced on a sliding scale, depending on the buyer's ability to pay.
- Avoid bending and stooping; long-handled reachers, dust pans, and any other tools that can be used from a standing position should be accessible.
- Use automatic shutoff units where available, such as on an electric teapot or the electric range.
- Organize the kitchen space so that often-used items are accessible, and repetitively used appliances, such as a toaster and a can opener, are easy to reach.

Bathroom

- Since getting in and out of the bathtub is a major safety problem, consider a large shower that has a fold-up seat but no curb; alternatively, purchase a bathtub chair, a bath transfer chair, or a bathtub lift.
- Install a raised toilet seat with grab bars attached to the toilet.

- Put down nonmildew short-nap carpeting—it's warm on the feet and eliminates the need for a bath mat that might cause tripping.
- Use a day-by-day pillbox or one with a reminder alarm; there are devices that dispense multiple medications automatically at a set time each day.
- Install a grab bar by the sink to hold onto for extra support.
- Put down nonslip flooring material, an essential safety hazard in this room where steam and moisture collect on the floor.
- Install a heat lamp; catching a chill after showering can lead to hypothermia.

Bedroom

- Add a bedrail for help in getting out of bed.
- Be sure there is a large-numbered telephone beside the bed.
- Buy a pressure-relieving mattress (either air or open-cell foam) if you are spending considerable time in bed.
- Mount a ceiling heating panel for added warmth.
- Wall-to-wall carpeting is safer and warmer than bare floors or area rugs.

Visual Limitations

As all of us age, our vision is generally affected in one way or another. Some of us can correct the deficiency with glasses, but another common experience is the onset of *low vision*. This term refers to a loss of vision that cannot be corrected with glasses, surgery, or other medical treatment, and it affects one out of eight older adults. Creating a safe home environment is extremely important for adults with low vision, since falls often result from simply not being able to see well enough to avoid obstacles.

There are four principal causes of low vision: glaucoma, macular degeneration, diabetes, and cataracts. Each problem affects eyesight differently as does, of course, the severity of the condition itself. Adequate medical counseling about the impact of the specific eye condition that concerns you can direct you to design choices in your home that will be helpful in alleviating certain problems. For example, glaucoma often creates tunnel vision, so items outside the direct line of sight, such as open closet doors, become dangerous obstacles. The Lighthouse National Center for Vision and Aging estimates that 90 percent of people with low vision can enhance their remaining vision by making special changes to the home and by using low-vision devices. The agency also can help locate low-vision clinics and support groups in your community. For information, call or write: Lighthouse National Center for Vision and Aging, 111 East Fifty-ninth Street, New York, NY 10022, 800-334-5497.

Indoor and Outdoor Living Areas

- Make all transition areas from inside to outside safe with extra lighting; the inside foyer should be well lit, and supply strong bright light outside the door as well.
- An intercom at the door lets visitors identify themselves, even if they can't be seen well.
- Outdoor paths and walkways should be well lit at night, and highlighted on edges with landscaping that creates a color contrast along the edges of the pathway.
- Replace round doorknobs with color-contrasted lever-action handles.
- Eliminate low furniture such as coffee tables and footstools.
- Move furniture against walls to create large area of uncluttered space in the center of the room.
- Contrast the color of the sofa and chairs with the wall and floor material.
- Light all stairs well, particularly the top and bottom stair; be sure the edges of the treads are taped or painted with a contrasting color.

The Alladin electronic magnifier.

• Keep an illuminated magnifying glass near any area where you read; a free-standing unit is particularly useful if your hands are not steady. For viewing prints or pictures, an electronic magnifying viewer with a color or a black-and-white monitor can increase print size up to fifty times.

• Enhance television viewing with a telescopic device available from a low-vision specialist; remote controls with large numbers; and a large TV screen, to place over the existing screen, which enlarges the image up to 50 percent.

Kitchen

• Outline the edge of the countertops with tape or paint in a color that contrasts with the work surface.

• Install full-spectrum fluorescent lighting under the upper cabinets.

• Use color-contrasted handles on doors, or use sliding doors on cabinets.

• Remove all unnecessary doors on cabinets.

• Purchase large-print cookbooks and a timer with large numbers; make enlarged photocopies of your favorite recipes.

• Mark settings on cooking appliances (such as *on/off, 375 degrees*) with visible nail polish.

• Select outlet wall plates that are color contrasted with walls.

• Purchase a cooktop with burners that are in color contrast to the appliance itself, such as black electric burners on a white cooktop or a halogen cooktop that turns bright red when hot.

• Buy a microwave with a sensor reheat feature.

- Use dinner plates with a raised lip—ideally, color banded around the edge—and differently colored from the table on which they're customarily used.
- Buy an automatic coffeemaker that makes a single cup of coffee; you won't need to pour boiling liquids and risk burns.
- Buy a chopping block that is white on one side, black on the other; you can chop lighter colored foods on the dark side and vice versa.

Bathroom

- Use bright tape to outline the toilet paper dispenser, the rim of the tub, and edges of the counter or vanity.
- Select a toilet seat that is a different color from the floor and the walls.
- Change light switch plates to illuminated ones.
- Replace any exposed makeup light bulbs around the mirror with glare-free lights.
- Color contrast all grab bars with the background wall.
- Add a waterproof light in the shower or the tub.
- Put automatic night-lights or wireless sensor lights in the pathway from the bedroom to the bath.

Bedroom

- Choose a bright bedspread to contrast with the floor, or sew a colorful ribbon around the perimeter of the spread; this will differentiate the edge of the bed from similarly colored flooring or carpeting.
- Use a talking alarm clock or one with very large numbers.
- Add automatic lights in the closet, and arrange clothes according to color.
- Install a sensor light at the bedroom door or an illuminated light switch, so you need never cross a dark room.
- Hang sheer curtains or blinds on windows to reduce glare.
- Attach contrasting molding or colored tape to furniture edges.

Impaired Memory and Thinking

Common causes for short-term memory loss among elders are stress, fatigue, grief, depression, or even medication. Generally speaking, with time, counseling, medical attention, and exercise, the symptomatic behavior lessens. Impaired memory and thinking, however, is an altogether different medical condition. Alzheimer's and other forms of mental impairment present particular challenges in environmental design. The disease often manifests itself in behavior that suggests forgetfulness, but memory isn't the issue. It is not a question of failing to recall where the car keys are, but rather an inability to understand what car keys actually are or what purpose they serve.

Dementia results in behaviors that can be dangerous to oneself and other household occupants, and oftentimes a caregiver must be constantly present. Even then, the safest course may be simply to limit access to rooms that present major hazards, such as the kitchen and bath. Because Alzheimer's and like diseases are so very difficult for both the patient and the caregiver, counseling is essential for family and friends whose loved one is not well. As with all progressive disease, a patient's requirements will change over time, and design solutions may be effective only for short periods before additional changes need to be made. An understanding of the medical condition and of the course it typically takes will ease the difficulties of living with dementia, and will facilitate an understanding of the environmental changes required to make the home much safer.

Indoor and Outdoor Living Areas

- **STAIRS:** Install handrails on both sides; this makes climbing easier; consider a wheelchair lift or a ramp, often required in later stages of Alzheimer's.

- **WALKING PATHS:** Agitation can sometimes be reduced by creating unobstructed wandering paths in the home; open doors or remove a wall, so a circular path is made. Alzheimer's patients often cannot turn around. Walking paths in a garden are also calming, but the garden should be securely fenced to keep the patient from wandering away. Check with a local nursery to verify that there are no plants growing in your garden that might be poisonous if ingested.

- **FABRIC AND CARPETING PATTERNS:** Choose patterns that are small and obscure; be aware that large swirling patterns can be seen as snakes or other frightening images.

- **TELEPHONE:** A picture phone with memory allows you to place your own pictures of family and friends under the transparent button covers. Manufacturer-supplied photos include police, fire department, or Red Cross photos or symbols. By pushing the picture, that person's number is automatically dialed.

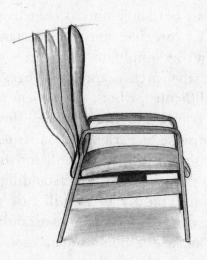

The Laurelwood, a stationary rocking chair by Sauder Manufacturing Company.

- **RUMMAGING:** Some people with Alzheimer's often rummage through drawers and closets. Keep a "rummage trunk" available and fill it with items that are safe to handle: old photographs, jewelry (without pins), trinkets, and scarves. Include items that are colorful, safe, and personal to the patient.

- **ACTIVITY CENTER:** Set up an area in the house where the two most therapeutic activities for Alzheimer's patients can be pursued: listening to music and painting. (Be sure paints are nontoxic.)

- **ROCKING CHAIRS:** Buy flat-bottomed rockers that cannot tip, to help discharge excess energy. Conventional rocking chairs are dangerous.

- **SAFETY:** Prevent wandering by disguising the front door with a mural on the inside, or install a musical alarm so a caregiver knows when the patient is leaving. Double locks can be installed, but due to the hazard of a fire, no occupant should be locked in a house alone. Some caregivers find that locks that are installed at an unusually high or low level will not be as noticeable to the patient. Windows should be locked and safety guards installed so that the window can only be opened six to eight inches.

Kitchen

The kitchen is potentially dangerous for Alzheimer's patients because dementia can create hazards that are almost impossible to fathom. No one would willingly ingest cleaning fluids, put their hand over an open flame, eat raw meat, or ruin appliances by using metal pots in a microwave. Yet these catastrophes are distinct possibilities if an Alzheimer's patient is left alone in the kitchen. Consider the following precautions:

- Install a main turnoff valve on a gas stove, available at a plumbing store, so the stove cannot be used without first turning on the main valve.
- Turn off the circuit breaker for the electric stove, or have a separate switch installed and concealed in a cabinet.
- Install childproof stove knob covers or remove knobs altogether.
- Lower setting on water heater so that the temperature never goes above 120 degrees Fahrenheit. Apartment dwellers can accomplish the same objective by inserting an anti-scald valve directly into the faucet, shower head, or the hot-water pipe below the sink.
- Install automatically timed faucets that will turn off if the water is left running; these devices are available from a number of manufacturers, including Chicago Faucet, and are available in plumbing stores and catalogs.
- Reduce the water pressure.

- Unplug small appliances when you're not using them, and install safety covers over outlets.
- Use childproof latches on cabinets and drawers.
- Camouflage the garbage disposal switch with fabric, or hang a box over it; alternatively, install the switch in a remote location or disconnect entirely.
- Limit access to the refrigerator/freezer by putting a lock on it.
- Use suction-cup dishware without patterns. High rims on the plates can be helpful in eating, as can two-handled mugs with nonspill tops.

Bathroom

Alzheimer's and like diseases progress in stages; some environmental design aids will be helpful for a period, then will need to be augmented. Often a person will deteriorate to a point where the purpose of the bathroom is no longer clear to them, and in fact, many patients are severely disturbed or agitated by bathing or showering. Planning a large bathroom is critical because in later stages of the disease, a wheelchair is ordinarily essential, combined with a great deal of assistance from a caregiver. Therefore, a five-foot turning radius is required, plus space for the caretaker to move about easily. In addition, depending on the severity of the illness, the following cautionary design features should be considered:

- Lock up or remove all medications and cleaning fluids.
- Cover or remove mirrors because they can be disturbing.
- Leave bathroom well lit at all times, and paint the bathroom door a bright, distinctive color.
- Tape arrows on the floor to point to the bathroom, or tape a picture of a toilet on the wall outside to act as a memory stimulus. It may eventually be necessary to remove the door and add a curtain that can be left open when the bathroom is not in use.
- Install a long-handled shower hose. By starting the shower slowly

at the patient's feet then working upward, the caregiver can keep the patient's anxiety level low.*

• Keep water pressure low and temperature to 120 degrees Fahrenheit maximum; remove plug mechanisms in tub and in sink.

• Install cleansing attachment on toilet; warm water and air are used to cleanse and dry, instead of paper.

Bedroom

• Bedrails should be installed to prevent falls; be certain the rails are closely spaced, to prevent other types of accidents involving entanglement.
• An electric bed will be useful in later stages of Alzheimer's, when patients typically lose their ability to get out of bed.
• "Bumper pillows" can reduce accidents that stem from thrashing about in bed.

The Lubidet hands-free cleansing attachment.

• A pressure-sensitive pad placed at the side of the bed or at the bedroom door can send a chime signal to a wireless receiver box. This will alert a caregiver to the patient's movements should wandering become a problem.
• Replace the footboard with another headboard at the base of the bed; this may reduce the tendency to crawl out of the bed at the bottom.
• Each day, lay out clothes in the order in which they should be worn, or do it the night before; put clothes in a wire basket, or hang them in a closet where no other clothing is stored.

* This and other useful suggestions for caregivers of Alzheimer's patients are found in the book *Homes That Help*, from the Architecture and Building Science Research Group at the School of Architecture and New Jersey Institute of Technology. See the bibliography at the end of this book for additional reference suggestions.

- Have patient wear an identification necklace or bracelet at all times. If it is removed at bedtime, put it with the next day's clothing. This precaution is essential should the patient become separated from the caregiver or wander off alone.
- Alzheimer's disease is often accompanied by incontinence; refer to the section on this condition on page 142.

Hearing Limitations

Hearing loss is a very frequent complaint among older adults, more often with men than with women. Isolation and loneliness are often a result when someone loses the ability to hear and to communicate. While new technology in hearing aids is helping many elders with this particular ailment, adults still rate their dissatisfaction with hearing aids as being higher than with any other assistive device. Environmental remedies in the home, therefore, are all the more important in improving the quality of life.

Living Areas

- A quieter environment will result from carpeting the floors, hanging lined draperies of heavyweight fabric, and using acoustical fabric on the walls.
- Air conditioners should be checked for rattling and unnecessary vibrations.
- Doorbells should be wired to ring in several rooms of the house; another alternative is a doorbell that flashes a light when rung.
- Smoke detectors should have both a loud alarm and a flashing strobe light.
- Amplified telephones increase total noise volume; the best amplification systems increase only the high-frequency range, which is

Flashing-light doorbell adapter.

generally more important. One company manufactures a product that allows the caller to speak to a local, toll-free relay service, where their message is typed and printed on the receiver's telephone view box. A flashing lamp unit can be hooked to the telephone to provide a visual cue that it is ringing. If you don't want to replace your phone, you can add a separate high-frequency amplifier and attach it to your existing phone.

• Use a television with a closed-captioned device; it creates the equivalent of subtitles.

• Arrange chairs at 90-degree angles or face to face for conversation with hearing impaired individuals; turn off all background noise such as radio and TV.

Kitchen

• If you are buying new appliances, choose ones that are well insulated.

• A wireless chime doorbell can be installed, assisting those with modest hearing loss; the transmitter is placed at the front door and the chime attached to the kitchen wall. For those with severe hearing loss, purchase a unit that also contains a flashing strobe light.

Bedroom

• Get a vibrating alarm clock; it has a unit that is placed under the pillow and vibrates when the alarm goes off.

Incontinence

Incontinence, a condition that affects women more often than men, is one of the major reasons cited for entering a nursing home. Innovative products for those who are incontinent are now available, however, that may make such a move unnecessary.

• Clensicair is a hospital bed with an air mattress covered by a vinyl filter sheet that suctions liquid waste and stores it in a portable basin at the bottom of the bed. Using a cleansing rod, a caregiver can bathe the patient and the filter sheet with a gentle spray of warm water. The water and the remaining waste are channeled away from the patient to the basin below; the filter sheet has a quick-drying surface, and the bed is equipped with a turn-assist function.

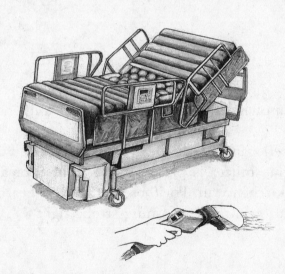

The Clensicair bed by Hill Rom.

• Dristar is a system designed specifically for women to wear at night or in a wheelchair. Liquids are pumped from an absorbent feminine-hygiene–type pad into a small box for disposal when convenient. The box can be placed on a nightstand or discreetly hung on a wheelchair.

• Techni-Floe's Medchair is an attractive wing-style chair specifically designed for the incontinent. Fluids are drawn down through a moisture-shedding fiber-core seat cushion into an absorbent pad on a hidden tray.

• Soft flannel sheets are available with rubber backing; they protect the mattress without being uncomfortable. Easily washed, they can be used alone or with a disposable underpad.

Allergies, Asthma, and Emphysema

About thirty-five million Americans suffer from upper-respiratory allergies, many of which, including asthma, are thought to be caused by allergies. There are probably as many types of allergens in the environment as there are people, but the most common irritants in the home environment are dust particles, animal dander, mold spores, and pollen. The optimal way to control allergies is to avoid or reduce your exposure to the allergens you know to be troublesome. This is more easily said than done if the allergen is something as common as dust, but frequent and thorough house cleanings are helpful. Other good measures include the following:

• Dustproof all rooms to the extent possible by removing wall-to-wall carpets, venetian blinds, and feather pillows. Better alternatives that don't trap dust are shades, washable curtains, and mattresses or seat cushions that are covered with zippered, plastic, dustproof covers.

• When cleaning, use a vacuum that is equipped with a special high-efficiency particulate air (HEPA) filter.

• Air conditioners can be helpful in preventing pollen and mold allergens from entering the house; portable units in individual rooms may reduce interior allergens, especially those from pets. Both central air-conditioning and portable units can be fitted with different types of filters designed for specific allergy conditions.

• Air-cleaning devices can be helpful in reducing airborne contaminants, including dust and pollen. They are installed either as in-duct systems or as stand-alone portable units. The Association of Home Appliance Manufacturers will provide a list of their certified portable air cleaners, together with information on the products that will help you determine the effectiveness of different models for your particular allergy situation. Send a stamped, self-addressed envelope to Association of Home Appliance Manufacturers Air Cleaner Certification Program, 20 North Wacker Drive, Chicago, IL 60606. Portable units have fans that, when operated at high speed, can be noisy. Be sure to visit a showroom and listen to a model in operation before buying one.

- When dusting, use a damp cloth.
- Keep the tile in the bathroom free of mold and mildew.

The Home Hospital

Medical breakthroughs, spurred on, in part, by economic necessity, have made it possible to treat conditions at home that previously required hospitalization. Doing so requires considerable information that is beyond the scope of this book, but if you are considering this option, I encourage you to research the topic carefully with professionals, such as the attending physician, a nurse association, and perhaps a spiritual counselor. For additional information, write for the free booklet, *A Consumer's Guide to High-Tech Home Health Care,* available from the Graduate School of Social Work/ Social Research, Bryn Mawr College, 300 Airdale Road, Bryn Mawr, PA 19010-1646.

In most cases, one's own home is the most comfortable place to recuperate from surgery, and even with a diagnosis of progressive disease, it is a more familiar, secure environment than an institutional medical center. It is now possible, when a dependable caregiver is available, to receive such treatments as chemotherapy, antibiotics, blood products, nutrition therapy, and renal dialysis at home. Some hospitals even offer telemedicine whereby patients are closely monitored by video camera and other computerized systems linked to the hospital.

To find out more about home care or to locate a high-tech home care provider in your community, call the National Association for Home Care

(NAHC) at 202-547-7424. Their booklet provides information not only about sources, but also about the feasibility of this alternative for different types of situations. If you are contemplating home care, first answer the following questions:

- Who will monitor the patient's condition? If family members are expected to, are they both willing and able?
- Does a supervisor from the hospital make periodic visits to observe hospital staff performance?
- Can the home care agency respond to any emergency twenty-four hours a day, seven days a week?

DESIGN CONSIDERATIONS FOR A HEALING BEDROOM

In setting up a home hospital room, organizational structure and tidiness are important, but the most critical issue is safety. The room should be clutter- free and, to the extent possible, noise-free. Think about making the room feel and look like a bedroom, albeit one with medical equipment, by using lively fabrics and bright, cheerful colors such as yellow or apricot. Music is restorative and therapeutic in many cases, so make sure there's a radio or stereo near the bedside. Whatever independence you can provide for the patient is also important, both for physical and mental well-being.

- Can the light switch be easily reached or has a remote control for the lamp been provided?
- Is the phone, emergency call button, or intercom within reach?
- Can the patient operate the controls for the bed?
- Are blinds or drapes wired for remote control so the caregiver needn't be summoned for this small task?
- Is there sufficient storage for all the necessary medical supplies? An armoire or standing closet can be bought so that an extensive array

Design features include an adjustable-height hospital bed, an armoire for storage of medical supplies, an overbed table for dining, and a personal emergency response system on the bedside table.

of emergency equipment or medication can be instantly available yet well organized and out of sight.

The bed is obviously the most important item of furniture in the room. Chapter 6 describes different mattress types, and one of these may make the patient a good deal more comfortable. More specialized equipment, such as a trapeze grasp or a patient lift, may also be helpful. Refer to the section "Mobility Limitations," page 114.

● **HOSPITAL BED:** Electrically operated to be raised and lowered for easy transfer of patients to wheelchairs, these beds also reduce back strain for caregivers. Attached side rails are available, as are attractive, decorative touches such as wooden headboards. Most hospital beds are rented locally through medical supply or home care companies. But one company, Sears Home Health, offers electric hospital beds that are available by mail order. They adjust from a flat to a sitting position and can also be altered for different heights.

● **MOBILE HOSPITAL TABLE:** This sturdy table rolls directly over the bed and eliminates twisting to reach for things located on a bedside table.

Be certain that the electrical supply in the room is sufficient to support the necessary medical equipment. Most home hospital equipment will need to be attached to a grounded outlet, and you should get the advice of an electrician before installing equipment. If you are responsible for someone in the home who is receiving medical treatment that involves high-tech equipment such as a home ventilator, you should call your utility company and any other community service such as the fire department. These agencies will then know that in case of a temporary power outage, an emergency generator is required in your home.

The Home Hospice

The hospice movement is founded on the principle that the last few months of a person's life should be as peaceful and comfortable as possible. For many, this simply means being at home, surrounded by loved ones, and not attended to in an impersonal medical institution. The most important practical consideration is pain management, while privacy and dignity are the spiritual goals that the hospice movement strives to attain. Many of the same agencies that provide home care also provide hospice care; services include nurses, homemaker chores, and spiritual counseling if desired.

Many activities that once took place in different rooms of the house and outdoors eventually will be centered in the bedroom, and the design features of a smart-aging bedroom (see chapter 6) are all applicable in a home hospice. Selection of a comfortable mattress is particularly important. If access to the outdoors is possible from the bedroom and if weather permits, a hospital bed can be rolled out to a patio. The bedroom should be kept uncluttered, clean, and quiet, and made as comfortable as possible for the friends and family who care for the patient. Guests will be grateful for a sofa bed or a cot in the patient's room or perhaps in an adjoining area.

CHAPTER 10

The Caring Community

CONTRARY TO popular belief, most older Americans are not isolated, lonely, depressed, or frail. Due to advances in our medical and spiritual understanding of the aging process, we have, as a society, the information and resources available to help us age with grace and comfort in our own homes. Though there is a statistical increase in the risk of disease and disability among seniors, an ever greater percentage of our older citizens is living healthy, productive lives, being vigilant about the types of exercise, diets, and lifestyles that contribute to their well-being.* In fact, the United Nations reports that "healthy, productive aging is being experienced by greater numbers of older persons" and that only 8 percent of the older people in the world are seriously impaired or reliant upon intensive health care.

* Draft Resolution, 1995 White House Conference on Aging.

At the family level, the local community level, and the federal level, more resources are available to assist seniors than ever before. Demographics, so tilted now toward a bulge in the population of elders, are partly responsible for this abundance, but so too is a new attitude that prevails about the issues associated with aging. Since so many of us now care for those who have already reached their eighth or ninth decade, we have been forced to reckon with our own aging, and in so doing, to reexamine our outdated views of the "stereotypical" senior. There is increasing acceptance of the fact that elders can be assisted to do a great deal for themselves, not cared for as dependent children, and that given the choice, total or partial self-reliance is every dignified adult's genuine preference. Even those who need a higher degree of care as a result of injury or illness still appreciate and benefit from inclusion in decisions that affect them so deeply.

The most fortunate seniors among us have large, extended families in the neighborhood who can provide all the assistance required, but even if geography has separated natural family members, there are a number of community services and support groups that fill a very important need— a need for the elder whose own capabilities may have lessened, and a need for the caregiver, whose own life is immeasurably enlarged by the gift of giving.

Finding Resources in Your Own Community

The best place to start searching for local resources or programs for elders is with an Area Agency on Aging; if you cannot find the listing in your neighborhood phone book, call the toll-free number in Washington, D.C., at the National Association of Area Agencies on Aging. This umbrella organization will provide you with the local number.

For the number of your local Agency on Aging, call:

The Eldercare Locator
800-677-1116
Mon.–Fri., 9 A.M.–9 P.M. EST

There are as many types of services for elders as there are needs. The following descriptions are by no means exhaustive, but represent the many types of support that in most communities are responsive to the needs of senior citizens.

HOME MODIFICATION, REPAIR, AND MAINTENANCE

The feeling of security and comfort in one's home is directly related to the adequacy of its maintenance. Still, many necessary repairs, however small, are difficult for elders to accomplish on their own. In recognition of this fact, many programs have been created by nonprofit organizations or by partnerships formed between private businesses and government agencies. Most, but not all, are restricted to seniors with limited income; for example,

- Christmas in April–USA, a national program with 162 chapters of organized volunteers in forty-eight states. This organization assesses specific problems in the homes of older adults and of low-income adults with disabilities. On the last day of April, trained volunteers complete the required improvements, then celebrate with a communitywide activity such as a picnic. This toll-free number enables you to find out if Christmas in April is active in your community: 800-473-4229.

• Even ordinary maintenance or housework can sometimes be too taxing for older adults, especially when heavy lifting is required. Local churches and synagogues often have housekeeping services available at special rates for elders.

In every state there are many more examples of programs for home repair and modification. The National Resource and Policy Center on Housing and Long-Term Care* has a useful sourcebook that lists virtually all of them: *The National Directory of Home Modification and Repair Programs* ($12.00). You will also want to evaluate whether financial assistance is available to complete home repairs.

GROCERIES AND MEAL PREPARATION

A smart-aging home has a kitchen in which elders can easily prepare meals, but not everyone chooses to cook three times a day. Some elders, recuperating from illness, may find themselves unable to cook at all. Meals on Wheels is a nationwide program that has assisted many seniors during a crisis or recuperation. Volunteers deliver one hot meal and one cold meal each day. Fees are on a sliding scale, with a suggested donation of three to five dollars per day. Meals on Wheels is listed in the telephone white pages or may be found through the Eldercare Locator number.

TRANSPORTATION

With as many activities as some communities offer, it would be unfortunate if there were not also transportation services enabling seniors to

* At University of Southern California, Andrus Gerontology Center, Los Angeles, CA 90089-0191. Telephone: 213-740-1364.

participate. In the suburbs especially, where distances are substantial, public transportation is often inadequate; and where it is adequate, often the transport vehicle itself is forbidding. Many public buses, for example, with their impossibly high steps, present serious difficulty for both young and old. There are, however, specialized services in many neighborhoods, and while finding them may require a bit of searching, again a local area office of the Agency on Aging should be helpful.

- **MINIVAN SERVICES:** Usually on a group fare basis, such services provide seniors with transportation to town or to the market, and some, on special request, will provide transportation to a doctor. Many such services receive government support and are, therefore, able to offer more competitive rates than do taxi services.
- **DRIVE 55:** This program is sponsored by the American Association of Retired Persons (AARP) for older adults who still drive and want to be retrained in the latest techniques on driving safely. Offered extensively in different parts of the country, this refresher course covers risks encountered on the road and how to avoid them.

RECREATION AND LEISURE

Adults who have been involved in community activities over the years know that aging need not deter their continued involvement in neighborhood programs. It is, nevertheless, important to evaluate whether a facility where social activities take place is a barrier-free environment, made safe for restricted mobility or vision. Some types of activities are specifically designed with the older adult in mind, and in such cases, both the facility and the programs are sensitive to the needs of their participants.

- **SENIOR FRIENDSHIP CENTERS:** These facilities for low-income seniors offer medical services by volunteer health providers, many of whom are retired physicians. The health care is offered within the context of many social activities, such as classes on current affairs, and it is designed to promote wellness through human contact as much as through reliance on medical intervention. Operated principally as "drop-in" centers for seniors, the facilities provide a supportive environment, particularly for singles or those without family in the community. The conceptual model for Friendship Centers began in Florida, but similar centers are now found in communities across the country.

● **DAY CARE CENTERS:** Similar to Friendship Centers, these facilities, which number more than three thousand nationally, offer programs to disabled or frail older adults. They are housed in a variety of structures such as churches or community centers and provide a range of activities such as memory stimulation or chair aerobics. Costs vary widely, from as little as twenty dollars per activity session to sixty dollars per day.

● **ELDERHOSTEL EDUCATION PROGRAMS:** Even for elders with a serious physical impairment, mental stimulation remains both challenging and rewarding. ElderHostel, having begun with a few colleges in New Hampshire, is now a program with nineteen hundred sites, conducting programs both on and off college campuses. The ElderHostel Institute Network also offers a program known as "Institutes for Learning in Retirement" (ILR), an open forum for learning in its participants' homes. Without grades or tests, ILR focuses primarily on personal development.

COMPANIONSHIP

In many situations, isolation rather than disease is a far greater risk for elders. Fortunately, there are a number of potential connections for older adults with limited social contacts, even when family members are geographically distant.

- **TELEPHONE SERVICES:** The local Agency on Aging is able to advise you on what programs are available in your area, but many communities have trained, volunteer groups that make daily or weekly calls. These regular "check-ins" provide a source of much-needed social contact for elders living alone, especially the frail, and are an important way to assess the individual's health and emotional needs on a continuing basis.

- **VISITING SERVICE:** Trained volunteers in these programs make house calls on isolated adults to provide social contact and to give the regular caregiver a bit of free time. The American Red Cross and Family Services Association generally can provide a volunteer visitor, as can most local places of worship.

- **AARP'S CONNECTIONS FOR INDEPENDENT LIVING:** This program focuses entirely on assisting older adults to live independently; it provides volunteers in a number of communities across the country. Members in the community volunteer corps try to address small but pressing needs of seniors with various types of limitations.

HEALTH CARE AND
LIFE-MANAGEMENT SERVICES

When family members are concerned about elders living in distant locations, it is sometimes wise to consider hiring a professional caregiver who can evaluate the needs of the elders.

- **GERIATRIC CARE MANAGERS:** These providers make daily or weekly visits, develop detailed care plans, coordinate needed services such as home health aids, and complete necessary administrative tasks such as submission of insurance forms. The services vary greatly in fees charged; it is, therefore, wise to evaluate more than one service and contrast their capabilities before making any decision. Contact the local Area Agency on Aging or the National Association of Professional Geriatric Care Managers.

● **BLOCK NURSE PROGRAM:** This program is the outgrowth of a government and foundation-funded effort known as "Reaffirming Citizen Power." The program leads national conferences to assist communities in identifying and responding to the needs of its elders. The operating premise is that life care at home benefits the total community, not only elders needing assistance. Collaboration among community nursing facilities, businesses, and professional agencies has built a support system in twenty-nine sites throughout the United States. Additional information on the program can be obtained from the Living At Home/Block Nurse Program: 800-320-1707.

● **NURSING HOME WITHOUT WALLS:** For Medicaid-eligible elders, this program operates in New York State, but many like it are operational in other states. Long-term home health care is provided at the same level as would be available in an institution, with an individualized medical program ordered by a doctor, and regular visits made by nurses, social service workers, or other health care providers. The best source for finding a similar program outside New York is the Elder Care Locator in your area.

Caring and Sharing in the Household

Sharing the resources of assistance in a community is an important source of interconnectedness for seniors; but on a much more individualized basis, another way to lessen isolation is to share one's own living space with others in the community. House sharing is not only emotionally gratifying, but also cost-effective and practical for many older adults.

There are various types of community arrangements that contemplate shared living spaces at the outset. Other "ad hoc" arrangements are becoming prevalent too, despite the frequent obstacle of unenlightened zoning laws. Women especially often age alone in large houses that they are reluctant to leave. Such advantages as sharing expenses, having someone present in the event of difficulty, and companionship through the long, cold winter months have encouraged many to consider some sort of shared living arrangement. The National Shared Housing Resource Center is an ideal source of information for ideas. An infinite number of arrangements are possible, but some that have been tested and have proved workable are:

● **CO-HOUSING:** Originating in Denmark some twenty-five years ago, co-housing is designed to bring people of all ages together in a living arrangement that offers both privacy and community. Members have their own living spaces, but, generally, share common areas such as kitchen, dining room, playroom or library. There is a strong emphasis on shared resources and close communal connections to all the other members. The model has been adapted in a number of ways in different geographic locations.

● **ASSISTED LIVING:** These centers, sometimes referred to as board and care homes, typically provide occupants with private apartments, complete with bath and kitchen. Personal care is available whenever needed, however, and a wide range of wellness programs or recreational activities are often made available on the premises. Basic shelter and services are covered in rental rates (starting at roughly $900 a month) with other services provided at additional charge.

● **SENIOR COMMUNES:** Less formalized arrangements than co-housing or assisted living are senior communes that often exist in renovated schoolhouses or very large single-family homes. Each occupant, generally, has his or her own bedroom, but other areas of the house are shared, as are maintenance chores and housekeeping tasks. Alternatively, a manager can be hired to supervise or complete household tasks. Some communes come together out of lifelong friendships, others out of shared interests.

● **SENIOR ROOMMATES:** Many seniors find living with a group of people too distracting but are happy to have one companion with whom they can share their house. In evaluating a roommate, be sure to consider emotional and personal compatibility. A systematic review of "house rules," such as which areas are shared, which private, individual responsibilities for chores, and a definitive list of "don'ts" (such as no music after midnight) will prevent painful misunderstandings. A contract detailing the living arrangement, one that is in compliance with local zoning laws, is usually the safest means to assure that both parties are operating on the same premise. A sample contract

---

Additional Information on Co-housing

Co-Housing: A Contemporary Approach to Housing Ourselves, by Kathryn McCamant and Charles Durrett (Berkeley, Calif.: Ten Speed Press, 1994. $29.95)

———

Fellowship for Intentional Community
FIC, RR1,
Box 155, Rutledge, MO 63563.
816-883-5545
The FIC provides the following:
Directory ($23.00)

Everything You Wanted to Know about Starting a Community, Audiotape
#C93-55 ($8.50)

Basic Ingredients before Starting a Community, Audiotape #C93-42 ($8.50)

called the "Housemate Agreement" TP#4.10 can be bought for three dollars from the Center for Universal Design.

Information Sources on Shared Housing

The National Shared Housing Resource Center may be a useful source for locating a roommate. Write to the Center at 325 East Twenty-fifth Street, Baltimore, MD 21218; telephone 410-235-4454.

Shared Housing for Older People: Planning Guide for Group Residences ($25.00). A practical guide for developing, financing, and managing a shared residence. Published by the National Shared Housing Resource Center.

Physical Space Remedies for Shared Housing

Not every house is ideally suited to the creation of private living quarters for another person, but a bit of imaginative renovation can often make separate accommodations workable. According to Patrick Hare, a housing and transportation consultant in Washington, D.C., 75 percent of all older adults live in homes with three or more bedrooms, and approximately one-third of all the homes in this country have space to include a separate apartment. Renovations generally require building permits, however, and these, in turn, must be issued pursuant to existing zoning laws, which vary dramatically from one location to another. Be sure to check with the local zoning board before considering one of the following choices. And if you find that local laws are not supportive of the needs of older adults, consider involvement in a civic association that advocates constructive change. AARP's free booklet *A Change for the Better: How to Make Communities More Responsive to Older Residents* suggests ways by which seniors can find a unified, effective voice within their respective communities.

ACCESSORY APARTMENTS: Adding an accessory apartment within an existing home may be either a comparatively simple undertaking or a major

building project, depending on the setup of the current home and the extent of the contemplated addition. The project may also entail consolidating living space for the existing occupant on one floor, leaving the second story for a younger, more energetic renter. If a kitchen or a bath on the second floor is needed, it may be wise to undertake other smart-aging renovations simultaneously (such as widening doorways to accommodate a wheelchair) on the first floor. This will lessen the disturbance of construction activity that is an inevitability in any renovation project, however competent and thoughtful the workers. To explore adding an accessory apartment in greater detail, call or write AARP for their booklet on the subject.

A compact kitchen unit minimizes the renovation needed when the second floor of a home is converted into an accessory apartment.

ELDER COTTAGES (ALSO KNOWN AS ECHO HOMES): These prefabricated units have been designed as barrier-free, energy-efficient units with ample consideration for the special needs of elders. Measuring approximately 500 to 750 square feet, an ECHO (Elder Cottage Housing Opportunity) cottage provides compact but complete living space with a bedroom, bath, kitchen, and dining area. The unit can be added to the side or to the back of an existing home, and even can be customized on the exterior so that construction details such as windows, siding, and roofing match the existing house. Many communities require that you remove the building when the need for the cottage no longer exists; the cottage is then dismantled, removed, and resold. When considering the addition of an elder cottage, be sure to evaluate whether your neighborhood requires a special-use permit or a zoning variance and whether adequate yard space will exist after adding an ECHO unit. The suppliers, Coastal Colony Corporation and Carmel Homes, can offer additional assistance in the planning phase.

HOMECARE SUITES: These units differ from ECHO cottages in that they were intended for insertion within an existing structure, though models are also available that can be placed alongside an existing dwelling. Designed by gerontologists and engineers as an alternative to long-term institutionalized care, HomeCare suites can fit temporarily into the space of an attached family garage and be completely ready for occupancy within seventy-two hours. The unit has its own systems for heat, air-conditioning, water temperature, and plumbing, but it is connected to the family's existing electrical and sewer system. All the important design considerations for an elder living space have been included, and options such as lift chairs, accessible bathtubs, and hospital beds are available for special needs. Financing is provided by the supplier on either a purchase or lease basis, with the expectation that the unit will eventually be removed and sold. Resale is also a service that the supplier provides for a fee. Contact Mobile Care, Inc., for additional information.

NURSING HOMES: Although many reasonable alternatives to nursing homes exist—alternatives that may in fact be superior—it is important to recognize that there still are situations in which the requirements of constant medical care suggest a nursing home as the most appropriate care facility.

Generally, a patient must be evaluated by a team of health care experts to determine if institutionalized nursing care is actually required. If it is, the patient should be actively involved in choosing the proper one. Research overwhelmingly supports the notion that if a person participates in the choice of a nursing home, their stay will be considerably more pleasant. I encourage you to review the resources that follow, as well as other books on nursing-home care that would help you make an informed decision if you or someone you love requires this level of care.

Additional Information on Nursing Homes

- *AGE PAGE, When You Need a Nursing Home*, available from the National Institute on Aging, 800-222-2225.
- *How to Select a Nursing Home*, available from the Nursing Home Information Service, 202-347-8800.
- *Nursing Home Life: A Guide for Residents and Families*, #D13063, available from AARP, 800-424-3410.
- *The Eden Alternative Directory*, available from The Eden Alternative, RR #1, Box 31B4, Sherburne, NY 13460, 607-674-5232.

For information on retirement communities, see the section "Moving On," in chapter 11 (page 172).

CHAPTER 11

The Action Plan

IF YOU'VE evaluated what you need in a properly designed house for smart aging versus what you have, and if you've audited your residence to identify the gap between problems and possibilities, you're ready to make some decisions and take action. But first you need to ask yourself the following basic questions:

1. Are the modifications required in your current home fairly modest? If so, do you stay in your house and make the necessary changes to improve it for smart-aging? Or are there reasons other than renovation requirements that might make moving a more legitimate option?
2. Do the improvements you need and want mean major renovation? If so, are you prepared, both financially and emotionally, for this undertaking?

3. If even massive changes could not meet your needs and your current home therefore seems inappropriate, what issues do you need to consider before moving to a new home?

Staying Put

If you've done your job properly, you've evaluated the smart-aging design deficiencies in your present home and analyzed your personal situation to identify necessary solutions, both those required now and those that can perhaps be put off for a while if necessary. If this process has brought you to the conclusion that you can make a few changes for maximum impact and that you need not worry about disruptive renovation or moving, you are very fortunate indeed.

Sometimes there are reasons to move, however, that have no relationship to the adequacy of your residence. Elders most often cite the desire to be near their children as a prime motivation for a move; other reasons are changes in the neighborhood, increased crime or street noise perhaps, or changes in lifestyle that require resources, such as a university library or a tennis court, closer to home. It may well be that the house is too large now and is far from public transportation. The time to think about a possible move is *before* a crisis situation makes the decision more complicated and emotional. If you've considered the choice carefully and believe that staying put is your best bet, here's how to get started with corrective action.

- First, make a list of the highest priorities. Broadly speaking, this ordinarily means those changes that will give you the most comfort for the least cost; but it also means those that address all *safety* issues.
- Organize the improvements by room.
- Make a separate list organizing the improvements by trade: If you need electrical work done, list everything that an electrician needs to

do, whether it's in the kitchen, bath, or anywhere else in the house. Do the same for the plumber and the carpenter.

• Then, tackle your list by first bringing in the tradesperson who has the greatest number of high-priority tasks to complete; this way you will have accomplished most of the corrective tasks even if you don't get all the way through the list right away. For complex projects involving several tradespersons, you will need to organize the workmen by the order in which their tasks need to be completed. For example, in a bathroom remodeling project, the electrician will have to install the wiring before the walls can be tiled.

• Make a list of all purchases you will need to make on your own; locate a home supply store or a gardening supply store that has a wide choice and as many of the items as you can buy in one place. Check the "Resource Guide" at the back of this book, too; many products can be mail ordered, or the manufacturer can often direct you to a retailer in your area that carries the product you want.

• If you can't tell a Phillips screwdriver from a socket wrench, now is *not* the time to learn. Delegate the entire process to a qualified contractor (see below for guidance in selecting a professional to work with) or a friend or family member whose proclivity for mechanical remedies has been tested and proven beyond any doubt.

Your home audit may have indicated that what you really need is furniture better suited to your current needs or perhaps strategic decorating with colors that will be practical if there is a vision limitation. If you want professional advice, consider hiring an interior decorator whose expertise qualifies her or him to provide smart-aging design advice. Personal referrals are an excellent way to find qualified designers; you can also call the American Society of Interior Designers at 202-546-3840 for a list of candidates in your area.

Apart from aesthetic design issues, there are trained professionals who conduct home audits for safety and accessibility. Occupational therapists, environmental gerontologists, and specially trained interior designers all can be helpful. Sometimes, a community service, foundation, or governmental agency will provide these professionals at no cost. Check with your Eldercare Locator (see page 151).

Renovation: Surviving It in Style

If your smart-aging solutions require substantial renovation, you need a much more detailed plan of action: a three-part strategy that begins with a list of construction changes, a financial plan, and a plan for surviving it without a nervous breakdown.

THE WISH LIST STRATEGY

If you've never built your own home and never undertaken a major renovation, you needn't believe all the horror stories you've heard. Good planning and careful decision making go a long way toward avoiding any trauma. Start with a list of what you would ideally like to have.

- Do you want to consolidate your living on one floor, add a smart-aging bathroom downstairs, and add an accessory apartment?
- Do you want to widen all the doorways for wheelchair access and to make the kitchen completely compatible for cooks and company of all ages and all physical abilities?
- Do you want to add a private patio off your bedroom and convert a small adjoining room to a large, well-designed bathroom?

Some dreams may be beyond your financial capability, others may be less costly than you think. Once you have an idea of what you would like to do on a large scale, you need to decide whether you want an architect to design the work, or whether the project can be managed by a competent contractor. Generally speaking, the scope of the job will determine your requirements, as will the talent of the people you hire. In either case, a professional will best be able to analyze the cost of the renovations you are considering.

When choosing an architect, contractor, or virtually any other trades-person to work on your home, the wisest choice is usually someone who comes highly recommended by a friend or family member. If there are reputable home improvement stores in your area, they too may have a list of tradespeople they can recommend. Absent any personal referrals, you can call the American Institute of Architects (AIA) at 202-626-7300, or the National Association of Home Builders (NAHB) at 800-368-5242 for suggestions.

Licensing requirements vary from state to state, but ordinarily, an architect must be licensed. In the case of a contractor, a license may or may not be required. Your local Home Builders Association (listed under "Associations" in your yellow pages) will advise you about licensing re-quirements in your area. But licensing is not necessarily a statement of professional qualifications or a guarantee that you will be satisfied with the tradesperson's work. The following tips will help you establish a good working relationship with your contractor from the outset:

1. Check references: Talk to several past clients and ask the following questions:

   • Did the contractor show up for work regularly?
   • Did the contractor finish the job on time and within budget?
   • Did he or she clean up the construction site at the end of each day's work?
   • Did he or she return calls to discuss problems?

- Did he or she inform you about any cost overruns or make suggestions en route?
- What were the contractor's greatest strengths?
- What were the contractor's greatest shortcomings?

2. Check for any complaints that have been registered against the contractor by calling your local Better Business Bureau or your state's Office of Consumer Affairs.

3. Get bids from different contractors and compare prices; obtain at least three written bids if possible. Contractors do not charge for a bid, but the quality of the items makes a substantial difference in price, and you must be certain that you are comparing apples with apples; be sure each contractor has identical plans and specifications. If there is a major discrepancy among bids, there's surely a reason, which you must discover. The lowest bid is not necessarily the one to jump at.

4. Check your contractor's insurance coverage—does he or she have liability coverage for both property damage and personal liability? Insufficient insurance coverage may compromise the contractor's ability to obtain local building permits. It may also leave you liable in the event of some mishaps.

5. Get a detailed written contract: Every purchase should be clearly detailed; both the start date and the completion date should be firm; be sure the contract states that all construction practices and techniques will fall within the framework of local building codes and standards.

6. Make the contractor responsible for obtaining building permits: This is a time-consuming process, but an essential one for which your contractor should be responsible.

7. Agree to a reasonable payment schedule: The customary fee schedule is one-third in advance, one-third halfway through the job, and one-third on completion. Never pay the entire fee up front, and never pay the balance before the job is finished to your satisfaction, including completing any inspection required by the local building authorities. Don't make changes in your plans without a written estimate of the change cost, and remember that every change costs money.

8. Include a method of conflict resolution in the contract: Arbitration and mediation are often better choices than litigation, resulting in faster resolution and less expense for both parties. If a conflict with your contractor does develop, be sure to state your position in writing and keep copies of your correspondence.

9. Cleanup: Be sure the contract specifies that the contractor must leave the working area "broom clean" every night. The contractor should also be responsible for removal of all construction debris.

FINANCING STRATEGIES

Once you've found the architect or the contractor you want to work with and have negotiated a reasonable price, you will want to evaluate your options for financing the renovation.

If you've sufficient savings or investments you can liquidate, the decisions are comparatively easy: Ask your financial advisor about which investments in your portfolio are the most logical candidates for sale. On the other hand, if your primary financial asset is your home, you still may be able to access the equity in your property to pay for the renovation.

HOME EQUITY CONVERSION PLAN: Assuming that you have paid for your residence and are not financially indebted in any major way, it is usually possible to borrow part of the value in your home even if you have no income. This option is known as a "reverse mortgage" or "equity conversion mortgage." Depending on the type of contract you sign, ordinarily you will have no required loan payments until the house is sold; at that time, you or your heirs will repay the loan from the proceeds of the sale.

It is comforting to remember that with most reverse-mortgage-type contracts, there is effectively no change in your legal relationship to your house; you are still the owner, able to sell when you choose, rent if you like, and make any cosmetic or structural changes you want. Typically, there are few if any residual financial claims on your heirs or on your estate even if the sale of the house does not cover the entire loan balance. There are also federally insured reverse mortgages available, so if the lender experiences financial difficulties, you will not be affected.

As in all financial matters, however, get professional advice and understand all the implications of the contemplated transaction. You should evaluate different options at different banks because interest rates will vary, as will the terms and conditions of each loan. Some reverse mortgages can be arranged as a line of credit, available for drawdown as needed, not only for house renovations but for other approved expenses such as medical care or even vacations.

If you are fortunate enough to have a good deal of equity in your present house, one of the wisest uses of those "savings" might be remodeling it to give you a safer, more secure environment for your later years. But before signing on the dotted line, be certain you are well informed.

---

*These sources provide reliable information
on equity conversion options:*

- *Your New Retirement Nest Egg: A Consumer Guide to the New Reverse Mortgages*, by Ken Scholen, director of the nonprofit National Center for Home Equity Conversion
- *Homemade Money: Consumer's Guide to Home Equity Conversion,* AARP bulletin #D12894

SURVIVING CONSTRUCTION

Few of us have the option of checking into a luxury hotel while our houses are being renovated, but you might want to consider staying with a friend in the neighborhood or with another family member. Living in the same house that is being remodeled requires considerable patience, a tolerance for chaos (or at least confusion), and an extraordinary sense of humor. If you think you're qualified on all three counts, you will probably survive to tell the story.

The most important organizational trick is to camp out in an area that is outside the construction zone and to move every single thing you need into this one area. Even if it's only two rooms—a den and a bath—it is manageable as long as you remember that it is a temporary inconvenience for an important, worthwhile goal. If your kitchen is being redone, you will need to set up as best you can in another area with perhaps a hot plate and small refrigerator; you will also probably do well to keep the telephone number of the nearest take-out restaurant close at hand.

A plastic sheet hung from ceiling to floor, then taped down during construction, will minimize plaster dust, but a thorough house cleaning is the inevitable end of any construction project, no matter how tidy your workpeople, nor how fastidious your housekeeping. Agree with the contractor in advance where tools will be stored at day's end and that the site will be at least broom clean when the crew leaves. For your peace of mind and that of others if you live in an apartment, set a reasonable daily starting and finishing time for the workpeople.

There's no question that you will be inconvenienced during construction, but being on-site will help you supervise and notice errors that are being made as they occur. Second-guessing the contractor every hour of every day will do nothing to improve your working relationship, but it is fair to ask reasonable questions periodically, especially if you notice work that you think is inconsistent with your design.

Moving On

If you have looked at your needs and your house carefully and intelligently, you may have concluded that the best way to live comfortably is to buy or to rent another home. Some construction projects are not worth undertaking, especially if the renovation is so substantial that it would be easier to find a different home. It also may be that the house in which you live is too large or requires too much maintenance to give you the freedom and leisure time you want. If so, give yourself the freedom to think about moving, without any pressure to do so if you can't find a new home you love as much as your current home.

If you're ambivalent about the idea, try to focus on finding answers to the following questions:

1. Are the people you love, friends and family, nearby, or would another home in another neighborhood put you closer to the people you most want to see?
2. Is the climate really suited to your current lifestyle? If you are newly retired and anxious to pursue outdoor sports or gardening year-round, would a different geographic zone be a better choice?
3. Has your neighborhood changed to the point where your safety and comfort are less than when you moved there originally?
4. Are you near the resources that matter to you—libraries, public transportation, shopping centers, good medical care?
5. Even if your home is familiar to you, is it really comfortable and safe? Are there more stairs than you want to climb every day? Do you stay home more than you really want to because negotiating snow-covered paths to the garage is more trouble than you can manage?

The idea of change may be unsettling if you don't know what your options are, but the best way to find out is to explore what's available. Organize your thinking by first deciding on the most suitable location. It's pointless to find a home you like in the wrong neighborhood. So identify where you want to be, then focus on the type of community suited to your needs.

Generally speaking, you can opt for either independent living—in a conventional home or apartment—or you can opt for assisted living of some type. Even if your present home is too large and its maintenance too demanding, you could move to a smaller home with less upkeep. Depending on how active you are and the state of your health, a community with all age groups and activity levels may be exactly what you want.

Alternatively, there are various levels of assisted living—offering supportive care to seniors whose needs may range from meal preparation and housecleaning, to simple "standby" help—assistance that is immediately available only when help is required. Continuing care retirement communities (CCRCs) offer all levels of support from independent living to virtual nursing-home care, usually in a protected community that is safe, secure, and maintenance-free for residents. Some older adults find that CCRCs and like facilities offer insufficient diversity of age groups, and that seeing young friends with small children in the community is a vital source of enjoyment. Others find that retirement communities are filled with people whose interests and ideas, given the similarity in their ages, coincide with their own, and that this commonality is the foundation for many new friendships.

Another important decision point is the choice to rent or to buy. Part of the consideration is financial, but a large part is emotional. If house care and maintenance are, for you, mere chores, a rental unit may be your ideal. The responsibilities for upkeep are largely those of the landlord, and your time can be spent on more pleasant pursuits than trying to find someone who will clean out your gutters each autumn. On the other hand, if home ownership is a source of comfort and satisfaction to you, look for a low-maintenance home, a co-op, or a condo that will give you all the pleasures of having your own place, without a high-maintenance requirement.

In any case, you need to concentrate your search on possibilities that will let you find as many elder-friendly features as possible. Don't think

"Aaahh, nice wallpaper"—this is a cosmetic detail. Instead, think convenience, safety, and peace of mind.

Assess different structures by simulating, to the extent possible, the way you would live in a place on a daily basis. Walk from where you would park your car every day, or perhaps from the bus stop, considering the distance to the front door. Ideally, there should be no stairs or, alternatively, a ramp should be provided. If there are stairs, make sure there are handrails and adequate nighttime lighting. Look at the building from the outside to decide whether there are too many obstacles to negotiate on a repetitive basis. Is the mailbox too remote, especially when heavy packages are delivered?

If you are looking at an apartment or condo, is the common area welcoming and well maintained? If the building is staffed, are the people at the door attentive and helpful? If you need to wait for a taxi on a rainy afternoon, is there a well-lit foyer with adequate seating space available? These features are not technically part of your own home, but they will have a dramatic effect on how much pleasure you take in living within the building itself. You can make many changes in your own space that correct small deficiencies, but in an apartment building or condominium, its overall management will dictate how comfortable you feel before you even get to your front door.

Once you're inside the building, look closely at interior features like the adequacy of storage areas for little-used belongings. Moving from a large home to a smaller one means less maintenance, but it also means less room. If you're in a shared building, the security system is another important consideration. It isn't only your own unit that must be safe, but also the entire building. The common hallways and doorways should all be reasonably wide and well lit if ever you need a walker or wheelchair. And while you're walking through a building that might be your next home, it is *not* impolite to look over the other residents to decide whether these folks will be friendly neighbors.

When looking at an apartment or a small home, remember you will probably want to have a bit of extra space for recreational activities or overnight guests. Don't try to live in a shoebox-sized space in order to reduce maintenance chores. Even if your worst memories are decades of weekends spent mowing endless lawns and battling incorrigible gophers, see if you can find a place that offers some access to the outdoors—a patio or balcony with a few potted plants or trees will bring maximum pleasure with minimum effort. Look, too, for an area of the house that can be a sunny "morning area." Many older adults find that mornings are far less rushed than earlier in their lives, and the opportunity to enjoy that leisure time in a pleasant space is more important than ever.

If you do decide that a move is worth it, you will find that some moving companies specialize in moving elders. Their services often include vital tasks such as evaluating whether your furniture will fit in a new place, packing supervision, and assistance in moving in and organizing your possessions in the new space. Administrative tasks such as changing your telephone and postal address also can be handled by these service providers. To find help in locating one, call the American Society of Interior Designers at 202-546-3840, the National Association of Professional Geriatric Care Managers at 602-881-8008, and Eldercare Locator at 800-677-1116.

Without extraordinary good luck, you are unlikely to find all the important design features you need in one space. Some smart-aging design solutions can be installed after you decide to move, however, even if you are renting. The Fair Housing Act states that landlords must not refuse tenants the opportunity to make "reasonable" modifications if they are prepared to absorb the cost of the changes. If you see that grab bars and other safety features are not included in the apartment you want to rent, talk to the landlord before moving in about any changes you would like to make; whether or not permissible by law, you do not need the aggravation of an argument with your landlord the day after you move into your new home! It may well be that the landlord is also familiar with new trends in smart-aging design and is more than willing to help.

If you decide that you want to open a new chapter in your life and move on, you must, of course, complete the current one first. As in all major projects, a systematic master plan is your best hope for anxiety-free closure. Discuss the tasks that your real estate agent feels are essential in preparing your house for the market, and remember that perfection in all details is not a prerequisite to its sale. Save your energy and your imagination for your new home!

Your home may be your castle, but when given a choice, rattling around in a drafty, turreted building with dimly lit rooms is not how most of us would prefer to spend our retirement years. A practical castle is what's desirable at any age, and I hope this book has enabled you to plan for your later years with functional designs that cost less than a king's ransom.

If you focus on the personalized ways in which you presently use your home and the things you do in it that bring you enjoyment, you can adapt the environment for the practicalities of your individual health profile, both for the moment and as you believe it will evolve. Still, the way you live will almost surely change as the years pass. One never knows when a much-loved grandchild will arrive to spend weekends, needing a separate room as much for your sanity as for privacy, or even when disability may strike. It is essential to understand that the way in which you now live— entertaining friends, visiting with family, immersed in your hobbies— constitutes the emotional heart of your home. Protecting your ability to live exactly as you like, no matter your age, is as crucial for your enjoyment of life as it is for the serenity it will bring to your family and friends, who will know you are safe and sound, living exactly where you choose—at home.

*T*HIS GUIDE is intended to advise you of the availability and, in most cases, the price range of some of the more difficult-to-find items referred to in the text. Some products are available by mail, some from several different suppliers. Be sure to compare prices, because they vary among vendors. Manufacturers' and suppliers' addresses and telephone numbers are listed separately following this list.

Product Resource List

AIR CLEANERS

Unit, portable and in-duct   Portable $200 plus; in-duct $3,500 plus
  Available from Honeywell and Sears Home Health

Bathroom Products

Bathroom, modular $12,000–$15,000
  Available from Robert Graeff

Bathtub chair, swivel $575–$625
  Available from Bathroom Access

Bathtub, with door $3,250
  Available from Kohler

Bench, transfer $90–$150
  Available from Sears Home Health, ILA, North Coast, and Maxi-Aids

Bidet, toilet attachment $400–$600
  Available from AdaptAbility, North Coast, and Toto

Chair, shower/bathtub $60–$70
  Available from ILA, North Coast, and Maxi-Aids

Fan, quiet exhaust $145–$280
  Available from Broan

Grab bar, bathtub rim $50–$70
  Available from Sears Home Health, AdaptAbility, and ILA

Grab bar, folding $83–$500
  Available from Smith & Nephew, Bathroom Access, American Standard, and Linido

Grab bar, toilet $35–$44
  Available from Enrichments, ILA, AdaptAbility, and Sears Home Health

Grab bar, wall hung $20–$40 (36" bar)
  Available from Linido, Ableware, and Crest

Hose, handheld shower $30–$220
  Available from AdaptAbility, Moen, and North Coast

Lift, bath chair $680–$1,600
  Available from Whitaker, Arjo, Smith & Nephew,
  and Enrichments

Multisystems, "Pressalit" $3,800 (sink, chair, toilet, grab bars, rail)
  Available from American Standard

Seat, shower folding $120–$225
  Available from Smith & Nephew and Bathroom Access

Shower stalls, multipiece $1,100–$2,800 (60" × 39")
  Available from National, Great Lakes Plastic, and Clarion

Sink, height adjustable "Pressalit" $665
  Available from American Standard

Soap dispenser, sensor $43
  Available from AdaptAbility

Valve, antiscald $20–$30
  Available from Perfectly Safe and ILA

BEDROOM PRODUCTS

Bed, adjustable height $1,400–$1,860
  Available from Sears Home Health

Closet organizer, carousel $1,450–$2,400
  Available from White Home

Closet organizers, wire system $6–$50
  Available from Container Store

Clothes, velcro $16–$50
  Available from Sears Home Health and AdaptAbility

Cover, pillow/mattress (allergy) $11–$65 (twin)
  Available from Sears Home Health and Self Care

Dressing aids $7–$14
  Available from Maxi-Aids, Enrichments, Sears Home Health, and Ableware

Handrail, bed $160–$170
  Available from AdaptAbility and North Coast

Hanger, extended $5
  Available from Fitz Hang

Mattress, air $300–$660
   Available from Select Comfort

Mattress, air overlay $120–$270
   Available from AdaptAbility and Crest

Mattress, open cell $532–$1,499
   Available from Tempur-Pedic

Mattress pad, "eggcrate style" $25–$31 twin
   Available from Sears Home Health and Enrichments

Oil, lavender $8
   Available from Joint Adventure

Pillow, cervical $20–$70
   Available from Sears Home Health, BackSaver, and Enrichments

Pillow, lower back/hip $60
   Available from BackSaver

Pillow, reading in bed $70
   Available from BackSaver

Table, overbed $100–$150
   Available from Sears Home Health, Enrichments, ILA, and AdaptAbility

Door Products

Door opener, automatic $1,200–$1,600 installed
   Available from Besam, NT Dor-O-Matic, and Whitaker

Doorbell, chime, wireless $20–$30
   Available from Maxi-Aids and Hitec

Doorbell, flashing light adaptor, Watchman "Doorbell Master" $60
   Available from Maxi-Aids

Doorbell, flashing light and chime, wireless $50
   Available from Nutone

Doorhandle, lever adaptors $10–$18
   Available from ILA, Maxi-Aids, Smith & Nephew, and Sears Home Health

Electric strike plate, deadbolt $150–$300
   Available from Hanchett Entry

Hinges, swing-back $25–$27
   Available from AdaptAbility and Sears Home Health

Key chain with light $3–$30
   Available from ILA, Lillian Vernon, and Sharper Image

Key holder, easy-grip $6–$10
   Available from Maxi-Aids and Ableware

Lock sets, lever/deadbolt $125–$300
   Available from Weiser, Ironmonger, Schlage, and Kwikset

EMERGENCY RESPONSE UNITS

Service, monitored $50–$80 (monthly fee)
   Available from Lifeline and Interim

Unit, telephone dialing $150–$280
   Available from Sears Home Health and Walter Drake

ENVIRONMENTAL CONTROL UNITS

Home automation, "Total Home" $4,500 (intermediate system)
   Available from Honeywell

Home automation, voice-activated $4,200 (intermediate system)
   Available from Performa Home

Remote control, appliances $25–$50
   Available from Brookstone

EXERCISE EQUIPMENT

Equipment, exercise $15–$50
   Available from ILA and AdaptAbility

FLOORING

Carpeting, nonflow backing $25–$35 (sq. yd. installed)
   Available from Collins & Aikman

Flooring, vinyl nonslip $4–$6 (sq. ft. installed)
  Available from Altro, Forbo, Armstrong, and Tarkett

Stair treads, vinyl safety $9–$10 (linear ft.)
  Available from R. C. Musson and RCA Rubber

HEATING

Heat panels, radiant $185
  Available from SSHC

Heater, wireless plug-in $40
  Available from Self Care and Home Trends

Thermostat, large numbered $36–$40
  Available from Maxi-Aids and Lighthouse

HOBBIES AND GAMES

Hobbies and games $10–$50
  Available from ILA, AdaptAbility, Smith & Nephew,
  and Lighthouse

HOUSEHOLD PRODUCTS

Cleaning utensils, long-handled $15–$30
  Available from Brookstone and Home Trends

HOUSING UNITS

Housing, "ECHO" $19,000–$36,000 plus installation
  Available from Mobile Care, Coastal Colony, and Carmel Homes

Suite, "HomeCare" $29,000–$35,000 plus installation
  Available from Mobile Care

INCONTINENCE PRODUCTS

Bed, bathing function, "Clensicair"   Rental (Medicare reimbursable)
  Available from Hill Rom

Chair, for incontinent users $600
    Available from Techni-Floe

Control unit, "Dristar" $2,200
    Available from Intermed Allstate

INTERCOM UNITS

Door chime & intercom, wireless $60
    Available from Sears Home Improvement

Intercom, video/door opener $1,200–$2,000
    Available from Aiphone and Honeywell

Intercom, wireless two-way $70
    Available from Home Automation, Hammacher Schlemmer, and Reliable Home

KITCHEN PRODUCTS

Bowl or dish, nonslip $9–$12
    Available from Ableware, Enrichments, and North Coast

Brush, with suction cup base $15–$31
    Available from Ableware, North Coast, Enrichments, and Home Trends

Cabinet/countertop, adjustable $500–$750
    Available from Accessible Designs

Cabinets, adjustable height $250–$300
    Available from Tavac

Cabinets, wheelchair accessible
    Available from Yorktowne and KraftMaid

Cart, adjustable height $135
    Available from AdaptAbility

Coffee maker, one cup $23–$27
    Available from Lighthouse and Maxi-Aids

Containers, nontwist top $30 (set of 3)
    Available from North Coast

Cookbook, large print $15–$20
　　Available from Lighthouse, Maxi-Aids, and ILA

Cooktops, electric $225–$300
　　Available from Kitchen-Aid, Frigidaire, Kenmore at
　　Sears Appliances, and Whirlpool

Cooktops, halogen or radiant heat $500–$900
　　Available from Thermador, GE, Jenn-Air, and Whirlpool

Cooktops, magnetic induction $900
　　Available from GE

Cup, "Thumbs-Up" $9–$13
　　Available from Maxi-Aids, ILA, and Ableware

Cutting board, black/white $20–$23
　　Available from Lighthouse and Maxi-Aids

Cutting board, one-hand use $17–$60
　　Available from Lighthouse, Enrichments, Maxi-Aids, and ILA

Dishwasher, above counter $400+
　　Available from Asko, Welbilt

Dishwasher, quiet operation $500–$850
　　Available from Jenn-Air, Asko, Kenmore at Sears Appliances, and Maytag

Faucet turners, lever adaptors $9–$20
　　Available from Smith & Nephew, Ableware, and North Coast

Faucets, sensor $300–$725
　　Available from Speakman, Cambridge Brass, Kohler, and National

Faucets, time-adjusted $300–$350
　　Available from Chicago Faucet and Speakman

Faucets, with pullout hose $266–$500
　　Available from Delta, Grohe, Rohl, and Kohler

Feeder, battery-operated $2,200
　　Available from North Coast and Sammons

Feeder, manual $150
  Available from AdaptAbility

Fire suppressant system $515–$750
  Available from Twenty-first Century

Foam, tubular $3–$8 (yd.)
  Available from North Coast and Sammons

Garbage disposal $75–$275
  Available from Thermador, GE, and Kenmore at Sears Appliances

Garbage pail, recycling $25
  Available from IKEA

Grater, with suction cup base $13
  Available from Enrichments

Holder, carton $3–$5
  Available from Lighthouse, North Coast, and Maxi-Aids

Jar opener, mounted $7–$10
  Available from Lighthouse, AdaptAbility, Maxi-Aids, and ILA

Kitchen, efficiency $3,300–$4,500 (laminate)
  Available from Dwyer and Cervitor Kitchens

Knife/fork, single unit $30
  Available from Ableware

Knives, rocker $10–$32
  Available from Lighthouse, AdaptAbility, Maxi-Aids, and ILA

Knob turner $13–$25
  Available from Ableware, ILA, Maxi-Aids, and Enrichments

Microwave, grilling feature $400
  Available from KitchenAid

Microwave, sensor reheat $200
  Available from Sharp Electronics

Mugs, two-handled $9–$12
  Available from Ableware, Maxi-Aids, and ILA

Pans, lightweight $25–$140
   Available from Lighthouse and Enrichments

Peeler, large-handled $6–$8
   Available from Maxi-Aids, ILA, Ableware, and AdaptAbility

Peeler, one-hand use $12–$40
   Available from Maxi-Aids, ILA, and Sears Home Health

Plate, scoop lip $5–$6
   Available from Ableware, Maxi-Aids, ILA, and AdaptAbility

Pot handles, cool touch $3–$8
   Available from Maxi-Aids and ILA

Pot lid adaptor $10–$11
   Available from Lighthouse, Enrichments, Smith & Nephew, and Maxi-Aids

Reacher $24–$40
   Available from North Coast, AdaptAbility, Ableware, and Enrichments

Refrigerator, side-by-side $800–$1,400
   Available from Frigidaire, Whirlpool, GE, and Sears Home Improvement

Sink, shallow $200–$300
   Available from Elkay, American Standard, and Kindred

Sink/cabinet, height adjustable $4,000
   Available from B. J.

Stool, safety handle $60
   Available from Hammacher Schlemmer and Chef's

Table, fold-up $80–$90
   Available from AdaptAbility and Enrichments

Tea kettle, automatic turn-off $22–$40
   Available from Lillian Vernon, Lighthouse, and Maxi-Aids

Timer, electric range $400
   Available from Logan Powell

Timer, portable with necklace $16–$18
   Available from ILA and Home Trends

Tipper, teakettle stand $33–$35
  Available from Smith & Nephew and North Coast

Toaster oven, convection $120–$225
  Available from Chef's and Welbilt

Utensils, built-up handles $6–$8
  Available from Enrichments, Smith & Nephew, and AdaptAbility

Utensils, nonspill $12
  Available from Sammons

Utensils, weighted $8
  Available from AdaptAbility

Wall oven $700–$1,000
  Available from GE, Jenn-Air, Maytag, and Sears Home Improvement

Wall oven, side opening door $500
  Available from Frigidaire

Washer/dryer, single unit $800
  Available from Malber

Wire shelf, closet $10
  Available from Home Trends, Container Store, Walter Drake

LIGHTING

Bulb, full-spectrum, chromalux $8–$9 (100 watt bulb)
  Available from Gardener's, Maxi-Aids, Lighthouse, and Hammacher Schlemmer

Desk lamps, nonglare $13–$320
  Available from Waldmann, Crest, Maxi-Aids, and Brookstone

Light, battery-operated $6–$11
  Available from Reliable Home, Home Trends, and Sears Home Improvement

Light, power failure $11–$20
  Available from ILA, Reliable Home, Sharper Image, Sears Home Improvement

Lighting control system $9,000+
  Available from Honeywell

Night-light, automatic $4–$5
Available from Crest, Tru-Value, Wal-Mart, and Kmart

Night-light, sensor $26–$30
Available from Brookstone and Home Trends

Remote control unit $30–$40
Available from Enrichments, Maxi-Aids, and Home Automation

Sensor light, table/wall $20–$30
Available from Brookstone and Sears Home Improvement

Switch cover $10
Available from Sears Home Improvement

Switch extender $7–$11
Available from Perfectly Safe, Maxi-Aids, and Access

Touch-turn-on unit $13–$15
Available from Maxi-Aids, Access, Enrichments, and ILA

Wall switch, lighted rocker $6–$8
Available from Home Automation

Wall switch, sensor $16
Available from Home Automation

Wall switch, wireless $33–$40
Available from Home Automation and Brookstone

Wall switch, wireless 3-way $33
Available from Home Automation

MOBILITY PRODUCTS

Cane holder and clip $4–$5
Available from Access and Ableware

Canes, hand-painted $35–$50
Available from Raisin' Cane

Chair lift, stairs $3,500–$4,600 installed
Available from Econol, Whitaker, and American Stair-Glide

Elevator, "Minivator" $12,000–$18,000 installed
  Available from American Stair-Glide

Handrail, vinyl-covered $60/(2) 6'-lengths
  Available from Crest

Leg-lifter strap $11–$14
  Available from Smith & Nephew and AdaptAbility

Lift, homecare $1,300–$4,700
  Available from Guardian, Nor-Am, Ted Hoyer, and North Coast

Lift, wheelchair $8,000–$12,000 installed
  Available from National Wheel-O-Vator, American Stair-Glide, Flinchbaugh, and Econol

Ramps, portable $50–$630
  Available from Sears Home Improvement, AdaptAbility, and Whitaker

Scooters $1,400–$5,000
  Available from Bruno, Sears Home Health, Electric Mobility

Seating system, "Jay Care"   Medicare reimbursable
  Available from Jay Medical

Walker, "U-Step"   Medicare reimbursable
  Available from Wenzelite

Walker, with seat $275–$400
  Available from Whitaker, Sears Home Health, AdaptAbility, ILA

Wheelchair, narrowing $2,000
  Available from Pathfinder

Wheelchair, Rock'N'Go $750–$900
  Available from Homecrest

Outdoor Products

Awning, automatic $2,350 (12' × 8' awning, installed)
  Available from Durasol

Bat house $30–$40
  Available from Gardener's and Sears Home Improvement

Containers, sensor $9–$150
   Available from Gardener's, Planter Technology, and Brookstone

Deck lighting, stairs $11
   Available from Toro

Decking/ramp material, "Trex"   5%–20% above pressure-treated lumber
   Available from Trex Co.

Floodlight, motion-activated $25
   Available from Home Automation

Flower boxes, deck railing $34
   Available from Gardener's

Light, solar $50–$70
   Available from Gardener's, Brookstone, and Sears Home Improvement

Photocell unit/individual light $10
   Available from ILA and Walter Drake

Porch screening system $180 (10' × 12' porch)
   Available from Screen Tight

Tablecloth, vinyl $15 (70" round)
   Available from Walter Drake

Timer, lighting $35–$65
   Available from Toro

Timer, water $65–$100
   Available from Gardener's and Brookstone

Tools, garden $10–$50
   Available from Gardener's, Access, North Coast, and Brookstone

Trellis/teepee kit $10–$50
   Available from Gardener's

Watering systems $22–$35
   Available from Gardener's

PILL ALARM

Pill reminder $15–$200
   Available from Tele Larm, Maxi-Aids, and ILA

READING AIDS

Magnifier, electronic $900–$3,400
   Available from ILA and Lighthouse

Magnifier, hands-free $20–$100
   Available from Maxi-Aids and Sears Home Health

Page-turning device, battery operated $625–$1,000
   Available from Touch Turner

RECEPTACLE

Receptacle, shock proof $10–$20
   Available from Perfectly Safe and Crest

SEATING

Back/seat, orthopedic (portable) $44–$83
   Available from Enrichments and BackSaver

Chair, "lift-up" recliner $700–$2,000
   Available from Sears Home Health, American Standard, Whitaker, and Mobile Care

Chair, with high seat $500
   Available from Rehab Seating

Chair, with rocking device $400–$500
   Available from Sauder

Chairs/sofas, for seniors $250+
   Available from Thomasville, Senior Style, and Primarily Seating

Lift mechanism, chair $395
   Available from Whitaker

SMOKE ALARM

Smoke alarm, lithium $20–$35
  Available from Sears Home Improvement

Smoke alarm, strobe light $25–$100
  Available from Maxi-Aids and ILA

TELEPHONE

Hi-frequency, adjustable $70–$110
  Available from Lighthouse, Maxi-Aids, and Sears Home Health

Picture button $50
  Available from ILA

Text and audio $170
  Available from Maxi-Aids

Voice-automated dialer $150–$585
  Available from Home Automation and Maxi-Aids

TELEPHONE ACCESSORIES

Overlay, large number $7–$8
  Available from Maxi-Aids, Lighthouse, and ILA

Ring alerter, flashing lamp $40
  Available from ILA and Maxi-Aids

Volume adjuster, hi-frequency attachment $40
  Available from Bruce Medical

TELEVISION PRODUCTS

Remote control, large lettered $15–$30
  Available from Lighthouse, ILA, and Maxi-Aids

Screen enlarger $70 (17"–23")
  Available from Lighthouse

Window Products

Crank and latch adaptor $300 plus installation
  Available from A-Solution

Drapery opening unit, automatic $200–$800 plus installation
  Available from Home Automation

Mylar film $21–$40 (roll)
  Available from Brookstone and Home Trends

Manufacturers and Suppliers

Ableware by Maddak, Inc. (catalog)
6 Industrial Road
Pequannock, NJ 07440-1993
201-628-7600

Access With Ease (catalog)
P.O. Box 1150
Chino Valley, AZ 86323
800-531-9479

Accessible Designs
94 North Columbus Road
Athens, OH 45701
614-593-5240

AdaptAbility (catalog)
P.O. Box 515
Colchester, CT 06415-0515
800-266-8856

Aiphone Corp.
1700 130th Avenue N.E.
Bellevue, WA 98005
206-455-0510

Altro Floors
467 Forbes Boulevard
South San Francisco, CA 94080
800-382-0333

American Stair-Glide Corp.
4001 East 138th Street
Grandview, MO 64030
800-925-3100

American Standard
P.O. Box 6280
Piscataway, NJ 08855
800-359-3261

Arjo-Century Inc.
8130 Lehigh Avenue
Morton Grove, IL 60053
800-323-1245

Armstrong World Ind.
P.O. Box 3001
Lancaster, PA 17604-3001
800-233-3823

Asko
1161 Executive Drive West
Richardson, TX 75081
800-367-2444

A-Solution, Inc.
1332 Lobo Place NE
Albuquerque, NM 87106
505-256-0115

BackSaver Products Co. (catalog)
53 Jeffrey Avenue
Holliston, MA 01746
800-251-2225

Bathroom Access (catalog)
P.O. Box 342, Cathedral Station
New York, NY 10025-0342
800-665-0246

Besam, Inc.
81 Twin Rivers Drive
Hightstown, NJ 08520-5212
800-752-9290; 609-443-5800

B. J. Industries, Inc.
2900 Wind Cave Court
Burnsville, MN 55337
612-890-3870

Broan Manufacturing Inc.
P.O. Box 140
Hartford, WI 53027
800-548-0790

Brookstone (catalog)
17 Riverside Street
Nashua, NH 03062
800-926-7000

Bruce Medical Supply (catalog)
411 Waverly Oaks Road
Waltham, MA 02254
800-225-8446

Bruno Independent Living Aids
P.O. Box 84
1780 Executive Drive
Oconomowoc, WI 53066
800-882-8183; 414-567-4990

Cambridge Brass
140 Orion Place
Cambridge, Ontario
Canada N1R 5V1
800-724-3906

Carmel Homes
P.O. Box 1698
Torrington, CT 06790
860-379-1989

Cervitor Kitchens Inc.
10775 Lower Azusa Road
El Monte, CA 91731-1351
800-523-2666; 818-443-0184

Chef's Catalog (catalog)
3215 Commercial Avenue
Northbrook, IL 60062-1900
800-338-3232

Chicago Faucet Co.
2100 South Clearwater Drive
Des Plaines, IL 60018
847-803-5000

Clarion Fiberglass
205 Amsler Avenue
Shippenville, PA 16254
800-576-9228

Coastal Colony Corp.
2935 Meadow View Road
Manheim, PA 17545
717-665-6761

Collins & Aikman
P.O. Box 1447
Dalton, GA 30722-1447
800-248-2878

Container Store (catalog)
2000 Valewood Parkway
Dallas, TX 75234
800-733-3532

Crest Electronics, Inc.
P.O. Box 727
Dassel, MN 55325-0727
800-328-8908

Delta Faucet Co.
55 East 111th Street
Indianapolis, IN 46280
800-345-3358; 317-848-1812

Walter Drake & Sons (catalog)
56 Drake Building
Colorado Springs, CO 80940
800-525-9291

Durasol Systems, Inc.
197 Stone Castle Road
Rock Tavern, NY 12575
800-838-7276; 914-778-1000

Dwyer Products
418 North Calumet Avenue
Michigan City, IN 46360-5019
800-348-8508

Econol Stairway Lift Corp.
2513 Center Street
Cedars Falls, IA 50613
319-277-4777

Electric Mobility
1 Mobility Plaza
Sewell, NJ 08080
800-662-4548

Elkay Products
2222 Camden Court
Oakbrook, IL 60521
630-574-8484

Enrichments (catalog)
P.O. Box 5050
Bolingbrook, IL 60440-5050
800-323-5547

Fitz Hang
17711 Metzler Lane, Suite A
Huntington Beach, CA 92647
800-409-4669

Flinchbaugh Company, Inc.
390 Eberts Lane
York, PA 17403
800-326-2418; 717-848-2418

Forbo Industries
P.O. Box 667
Hazleton, PA 18201
800-842-7839

Frigidaire Co.
6000 Perimeter Drive
Dublin, OH 43017
800-685-6005

Gardener's Supply Co. (catalog)
128 Intervale Road
Burlington, VT 05401-2850
802-863-1700

GE Appliances
Appliance Park
Louisville, KY 40225
800-626-2000

Professor Robert Graeff
1080 North Milwaukee Avenue
Chicago, IL 60622
312-276-9157

Great Lakes Plastic
P.O. Box 600
Hancock, MI 49930
906-482-3750

Grohe America, Inc.
241 Covington Drive
Bloomingdale, IL 60108
630-582-7711

Guardian (Div. of Sun Med)
4175 Guardian Street
Simi Valley, CA 93063
800-255-5022

Hammacher Schlemmer (catalog)
9180 Le Saint Drive
Fairfield, OH 45014-5475
800-543-3366

Hanchett Entry Systems
2040 West Quail Avenue
Phoenix, AZ 85027
800-626-7590; 602-957-2472

Hill Rom
4349 Corporate Road
Charleston, SC 29405
800-845-2478

Hitec Group International, Inc.
8160 Madison
Burr Ridge, IL 60521
800-288-8303

Home Automation Systems, Inc.
(catalog)
151 Kalmus Drive, Suite L4
Costa Mesa, CA 92626
800-762-7846

Homecrest Industries, Inc.
P.O. Box 350
Wadena, MN 56482
800-346-4852

Home Trends (catalog)
1450 Lyell Avenue
Rochester, NY 14606-2184
716-254-6520

Honeywell, Inc.
1985 Douglas Drive North
Golden Valley, MN 55422-3992
800-345-6770

Ted Hoyer & Co., Inc.
222 Minnesota Street
Oshkosh, WI 54903
414-231-7970

IKEA Service Office
Plymouth Meeting Hall
498 W. Germantown Pike
Plymouth, PA 19462
800-434-4532

ILA: Independent Living Aids
(catalog)
27 East Mall
Plainview, NY 11803
800-537-2118

In-Step Mobility Products, Inc.
3306 West Lee Street
Skokie, IL 60076
800-558-7837

Intermed Allstate
14001 Ridgedale Drive
Minnetonka, MN 55305
800-328-2915

Interim Healthcare
4411 Mercury, Suite 206
San Diego, CA 92111
800-308-6656

Ironmonger
122 West Illinois Street
Chicago, IL 60610-4506
800-621-1937

Jay Medical Ltd.
P.O. Box 18656
Boulder, CO 80308
800-648-8282

Jenn-Air (Div. of Maytag)
240 Edward Street
Cleveland, TN 37311
800-688-1100

Joint Adventure (catalog)
P.O. Box 824
Rogers, AR 72757
800-898-PURE

Kindred Ind.
P.O. Box 190
Midland, Ontario
Canada L4R4K9
800-465-5586

KitchenAid (Div. of Whirlpool)
701 Main Street
Saint Joseph, MI 49085
800-253-3977

Kohler Co.
444 Highland Drive
Kohler, WI 53044
800-456-4537; 414-457-4441

KraftMaid
16052 Industrial Parkway
Middlefield, OH 44062
800-462-6931

Lifeline
640 Memorial Drive
Cambridge, MA 02139-4851
800-543-3574

**Lighthouse Consumer Products
(catalog)**
36-20 Northern Boulevard
Long Island City, NY 11101
800-829-0500

Lillian Vernon (catalog)
2600 International Parkway
Virginia Beach, VA 23452
800-285-5555

Linido USA
1090 McCallie Avenue
Chattanooga, TN 37404
800-698-4504

Logan Powell Co.
2415-A Old Gettysburg Road
Camp Hill, PA 17011
717-730-2671

Malber U.S.A., Inc.
1999 Grand Avenue
Baldwin, NY 11510
800-600-8913; 516-377-1865

Maxi-Aids (catalog)
P.O. Box 3209
Farmingdale, NY 11735
800-522-6294

Maytag/Admiral Products
One Dependability Square
Newton, IA 50208
515-792-7000

Mobile Care Inc.
P.O. Box 489
Great Bend, KS 67530
800-383-9090; 316-793-5462

Moen Inc.
25300 Al Moen Drive
North Olmsted, OH 44070-8022
800-553-6636

R. C. Musson Rubber Co.
1320 East Archwood Avenue
Akron, OH 44306
800-321-2381

National Fiber Glass Products
5 Greenwood Avenue
Romeoville, IL 60446-1398
815-886-5900

National Wheel-O-Vator Co.
509 West Front Street
Roanoke, IL 61561
800-782-1222

Nor-Am Patient Care Products Ltd.
P.O. Box 543
Lewiston, NY 14092
800-387-7103; 716-285-7548

North Coast Medical, Inc. (catalog)
P.O. Box 6070
San Jose, CA 95150
800-235-7054

NT Dor-O-Matic, Inc.
7350 West Wilson Avenue
Harwood Heights, IL 60656-4786
800-543-4635

Nutone
P.O. Box 1580
Cincinnati, OH 45201-1580
513-527-5100

Pathfinder Enterprises, Inc.
P.O. Box 7126
Gainsville, FL 32605
352-337-0234

Perfectly Safe (catalog)
7835 Freedom Avenue, NW
North Canton, OH 44720
800-837-5437

Performa Home
317 Highway 620 South
Austin, TX 78734
800-944-6873

Planter Technology
999 Independence Avenue
Mountain View, CA 94043-2302
800-542-2282; 415-962-8982

Primarily Seating (sold through designers and architects)
475 Park Avenue, Suite 3A
New York, NY 10022
212-838-2588

Raisin' Cane, Inc.
P.O. Box 535
205 Walden Street
Cambridge, MA 02140
617-497-6615

RCA Rubber Co.
1833 East Market Street
Akron, OH 44305
330-784-1291

Rehab Seating Systems, Inc.
Eight Alton Place, Suite 3
Brookline, MA 02146
800-525-7328

Reliable Home Office (catalog)
P.O. Box 1501
Ottawa, IL 61350-9916
800-869-6000

Rohl Corporation
1559 Sunland Lane
Costa Mesa, CA 92626
800-777-9762

Sammons Preston (catalog)
P.O. Box 5071
Bolingbrook, IL 60440-5071
800-323-5547

Sauder Manufacturing Co.
930 West Barre Road
Archbold, OH 43502-0230
800-537-1530

Schlage Lock Co.
2401 Bayshore Boulevard
San Francisco, CA 94134
415-467-1100

Screen Tight
407 Saint James Street
Georgetown, SC 29440
800-768-7325

Sears Home Health Care (catalog)
9804 Chartwell Drive
Dallas, TX 75243
800-326-1750

Sears Home Improvement and Appliances (catalog)
Hanover, PA 17333-0093
800-372-5282

Select Comfort
6105 Trenton Lane North
Minneapolis, MN 55442
800-344-6561

Self Care Catalog
104 Challenger Drive
Portland, TN 37148
800-345-3371

Senior Style
P.O. Box 69628
Portland, OR 97201
503-244-1719

Sharp Electronics Corp.
Sharp Plaza
Mahwah, NJ 07430-2135
800-BE-SHARP

Sharper Image
650 Davis Street
San Francisco, CA 94111
800-344-4444

Smith & Nephew Rehabilitation
P.O. Box 1005
Germantown, WI 53022-8205
800-558-8633

Speakman
P.O. Box 191
Wilmington, DE 19899-0191
302-764-9100

SSHC, Inc.
146 Elm Street
Old Saybrook, CT 06475
860-388-3848

Tarkett, Inc.
800 Lanidex Plaza
Parsippany, NJ 07054
610-266-5500

Tavac Manufacturing
10 Estill Hammock Road
Tybee Island, GA 31328
800-476-9025

Techni-Floe, Inc.
710 West Farrell Street
Niota, TN 37822
423-568-2381

Tele Larm, Inc.
4300 Six Forks Road, Suite 140
Raleigh, NC 27609
800-835-5276

Tempur-Pedic
848G Nandino Boulevard
Lexington, KY 40511
800-886-6466

Thermador
5551 McFadden Avenue
Huntington Beach, CA 92649
800-735-4328

Thomasville Furniture Contract
P.O. Box 339
Thomasville, NC 27361
800-225-0265; 919-472-4000

The Toro Company
5300 Shoreline Boulevard
Mound, MN 55364
800-321-8676

Toto Kiki USA, Inc.
415 West Taft Avenue
Orange, CA 92665
714-282-8686

Touch Turner
443 View Ridge Drive
Everett, WA 98203
206-252-1541

Trex Co.
20 South Cameron Street
Winchester, VA
800-289-8739

Twenty-first Century
3249 West Story Road
Irving, TX 75038
800-786-2178

Waldmann Lighting
9 West Century Drive
Wheeling, IL 60090
800-634-0007; 847-520-1060

Weiser Lock
6700 Weiser Lock Drive
Tucson, AZ 85746
800-677-5625

Welbilt Appliance Corp.
175 Community Drive
Great Neck, NY 11021
516-773-0300

Wenzelite Medical Supply Corp.
220 Thirty-sixth Street
Brooklyn, NY 11232
800-706-9255; 718-768-8002

Whirlpool Corp.
Administrative Center
2000 M-63 North
Benton Harbor, MI 49022-2692
800-253-1301

Whitaker Co. (catalog)
1 Odell Plaza
Yonkers, NY 10703
800-445-4387

White Home Products, Inc.
P.O. Box 340
Smyrna, GA 30081
770-431-0900

Yorktowne Cabinets
P.O. Box 231
Red Lion, PA 17356
717-244-4011

BIBLIOGRAPHY

CHAPTER 1. HOME IS WHERE THE HEART IS

AARP. *Understanding Senior Housing for the 1990's*. Washington, D.C.: American Association of Retired Persons, 1990.

Callanan, J., ed. "Aging in Place." *Generations* 16, no. 2 (1992). (Entire issue.)

Hayflick, Leonard. *How and Why We Age*. New York: Ballantine Books, 1994.

National Institutes of Health. *Research for a New Age*. Washington, D.C.: NIH publication no. 93-1129, 1993.

Official White House Conference on Aging. *Draft Resolutions*. Washington, D.C., 1995.

Tauber, C. *Sixty-Five Plus in America*. Washington, D.C.: GPO, 1993.

CHAPTER 2. DESIGNING FOR A LIFETIME

Adaptive Environment Center. *Consumer Guide to Home Adaptation*. Boston: Adaptive Environment Center, 1993, $12.50. (374 Congress St., Suite 301, Boston, MA 02210. 617-965-1225.)

AARP. *Facts About Older Women: Housing and Living Arrangements*, #D12880. Washington, D.C.: American Association of Retired Persons, 1991.

American Society on Aging and the National Forum on Technology and Aging. "Appropriate Technology for an Aging Society." Report based on the Technology and Aging Conference, Washington, D.C., November 17–18, 1987 (31 pages).

NAHB National Research Center. *Reducing Fire-Related Injury and Death Among the Elderly*. Upper Marlboro, Md.: NAHB National Research Center, 1990.

Pynoos, J., and E. Cohen. *Home Safety Guide for Older People: Check It Out/Fix It Up*. Washington, D.C.: Serif Press, 1991, 66 pp., $13.95. (1331 H St. NW, Washington, D.C. 20005. 202-737-4650.)

Rickman, L. *A Comprehensive Approach to Retrofitting Homes for a Lifetime*. Upper Marlboro, Md.: NAHB Research Center, 1991, 82 pp., $10 and $4. (400 Prince George's Blvd., Upper Marlboro, MD 20774. 301-249-4000.)

U.S. Consumer Product Safety Commission. *Your Home Fire Safety Checklist*, publication no. 341C. Washington, D.C.: GPO, 1992. Send 50 cents to R. Woods, Consumer Information Center, P.O. Box 100, Pueblo, CO 81002.

U.S. Department of Education. *Consensus Statement*. National Institute on Disability and Rehabilitation Research, vol. 1, no. 4 (January 1993), Washington, D.C. (28-page booklet).

CHAPTER 3: SAFETY AND SECURITY IN THE SMART-AGING HOME

AARP. *How to Protect Your Home*, #D395. Washington, D.C.: American Association of Retired Persons, 1990.

Metropolitan Center for Independent Living. *How to Build Ramps for Home Accessibility*. Saint Paul, Minn.: Metropolitan Center For Independent Living, 1993, $10. (1600 University Avenue West, Saint Paul, MN 55104-3825. 612-646-8342.)

Roschko, B. A. *Housing Interiors for the Disabled & Elderly*. New York: Van Nostrand Reinhold, 1991.

Tinetti, M. E., et al. "A multifactorial intervention to reduce the risk of falling among elderly people living in the community." *The New England Journal of Medicine* 331 (1994): 821–27.

CHAPTER 4. LIVING ROOMS AND ACTIVITY CENTERS

Liebrock, S., and S. Behar. *Beautiful Barrier Free: A Visual Guide to Accessibility*. New York: Van Nostrand Reinhold, 1993.

Roschko, B. A. *Housing Interiors for the Disabled & Elderly*. New York: Van Nostrand Reinhold, 1991.

CHAPTER 5. GARDENS AND OUTDOOR SPACES

Knox, G., ed. *Your Yard*. Des Moines: Better Homes and Gardens, 1984.

Ray, Richard, ed. *Container and Hanging Gardens*. San Francisco: Ortho Books, 1975.

Yoeman, K. *Able Gardener: Overcoming Barriers of Age and Physical Limitation*. Pownal, Vt.: Storey Communications, 1992. (25 Schoolhouse Rd., Pownal, VT 05261. 800-441-5700.)

CHAPTER 6. THE SMART-AGING BEDROOM

National Institute on Aging. "Pumping Iron Improves Strength, Mobility of 80–90 Year-Olds." *Research Bulletin* (November 1994): 3–5. Bethesda, Md.

Wylde, M., A. Baron-Robbins, and S. Clark. *Building for a Lifetime*. Newtown, Conn.: Taunton Press, 1994.

CHAPTER 7. THE SMART-AGING KITCHEN

Moore, L., and E. Ostrander. *In Support of Mobility: Kitchen Design for Independent Older Adults*. New York: Cornell University, 1992.

NAHB National Research Center. *Reducing Fire-Related Injury and Death Among the Elderly*. Upper Marlboro, Md.: NAHB National Research Center, 1990.

Wylde, M., A. Baron-Robbins, and S. Clark. *Building for a Lifetime*. Newtown, Conn.: Taunton Press, 1994.

Chapter 8. The Smart-Aging Bathroom

Graeff, R. "Bathroom Design for the Elderly." In J. Pirkl's *Transgenerational Design: Products for an Aging Population*. New York: Van Nostrand Reinhold, 1994.

Liebrock, S., and S. Behar. *Beautiful Barrier Free: A Visual Guide to Accessibility*. New York: Van Nostrand Reinhold, 1993.

Mace, Ron. *The Accessible Housing Design File*. New York: Van Nostrand Reinhold, 1991.

Steinfeld, E. E-mail correspondence on grab bars. Professor of Architecture, Department of Architecture, State University of New York, Buffalo. September 26, 1996.

Wylde, M., A. Baron-Robbins, and S. Clark. *Building for a Lifetime*. Newtown, Conn.: Taunton Press, 1994.

Chapter 9. Designing for Specific Physical Conditions

Corinne Dolan Alzheimer Center. *Home Modifications: Responding to Dementia*. Chardon, Ohio: The Research Center of the Corinne Dolan Alzheimer Center at Heather Hill, 1990, $4.25. (12340 Bass Lake Rd., Chardon, OH 44024. 216-621-8560.)

Faye, E., and C. Stuen, eds. *The Aging Eye and Low Vision*. New York: The Lighthouse Inc., 1992.

"Geriatric Occupational, Physical, Speech Therapies Module." Conference sponsored by Columbia University–New York Geriatric Educational Center, New York City, June 1996.

Kaye, L., and J. Davitt. *High-Tech Home Health Care*. Bryn Mawr, Pa.: Graduate School of Social Work and Social Research, Bryn Mawr College, 1994.

Mann, W., et al. "Environmental Problems in Homes of Elders with Disabilities." *Occupational Therapy Journal of Research* 14, no. 3 (Summer 1994): 191–211.

National Institutes of Health. *Something in the Air about Airborne Allergens*. Washington, D.C.: NIH publication no. 93-493, March 1993.

Olsen, R., E. Ehrenkrantz, and B. Hutchings. *Homes That Help*. Newark, N.J.: New Jersey Institute of Technology Press, 1993. (NJIT, Architecture and Building Science, University Heights, Newark, NJ 07102-1982. 201-596-8439.)

Saxon, S., and M. J. Etten. *Physical Change and Aging*. New York: Tiresias Press, 1994.

"Technology, Care and Living Environments." Symposium presented by the Stein Foundation and Stein Gerontological Institute of the Miami Jewish Home and Hospital for the Aged, University of Florida, American Association of Homes and Services for the Aging, and the International Association of Homes and Services for the Aging. Conducted at the World Conference on Independent Living, Orlando, Fla., November 1994.

U.S. Department of Education. *Consensus Statement*. National Institute on Disability and Rehabilitation Research, no. 4 (January 1993). Washington, D.C. (28 pages).

U.S. Department of Health and Human Services Public Health Service. *Consumer Version Clinical Practice Guidelines: Recovering after a Stroke*. Washington, D.C.: Agency for Health Care Policy and Research Publications Clearinghouse, publication no. 95-0664, May 1995.

University of California. *Home Safety for the Alzheimer's Patient*, catalog no. A-11. La Jolla: University of California, San Diego, 1989 (31 pages).

CHAPTER 10. THE CARING COMMUNITY

AARP. *A Consumer's Guide to Homesharing*, no. D12774. Washington, D.C.: American Association of Retired Persons, 1992.

AARP. *Expanding Housing Choices for Older People*. Conference papers and recommendations. Washington, D.C.: American Association of Retired Persons, 1995.

Callanan, J., ed. "Aging in Place." *Generations* 16, no. 2 (1992). (Entire issue.)

CHAPTER 11. THE ACTION PLAN

Rickman, L. *A Comprehensive Approach to Retrofitting Homes for a Lifetime*. Upper Marlboro, Md.: NAHB Research Center, 1991, 82 pp., $10 and $4. (400 Prince George's Blvd., Upper Marlboro, MD 20774. 301-249-4000.)

And More . . .

PUBLICATIONS

Branson, Gary. *The Complete Guide to Barrier-Free Housing*. Crozet, Va.: Betterway Publications, 1991. Available from: P.O. Box 219, Crozet, VA 22932; $14.95.

Caring for the Caregiver: A Guide to Living with Alzheimer's Disease. Morris Plains, NJ: Parke-Davis, 1994 (171 pages). Available free by calling 800-223-0432.

Home Modification Resource Guide. Los Angeles, Calif.: National Resource and Policy Center on Housing and Long-Term Care, 1996. Available from: National Resource and Policy Center on Housing and Long-Term Care, University of Southern California, Andrus Gerontology Center, Los Angeles, CA 90089-0191; telephone 213-740-1364; $12.00

Mann, William. *The Eden Alternative*. Sherburne, N.Y.: The Eden Alternative. This volume discusses the humanizing philosophy of Dr. William Thomas, whose views about nursing-home care have been recognized as particularly enlightened; $20.00, plus $3.00 shipping and handling. Also available is *The Eden Alternative Directory*, which lists nursing homes that embrace the Eden Alternative philosophy; free. Both available from: The Eden Alternative, RR 1, Box 31B4, Sherburne, NY 13460; telephone 607-674-5232.

VIDEOS

For the Rest of Your Life. A 28-minute video featuring a wide range of home adaptations for older adults. Available for a one-month loan from: The Hartford, 200 Executive Boulevard, Fourth Floor, Southington, CT 06489; telephone 860-276-8940.

Video Respite. This series of video tapes was developed by researchers at the University of Utah for cognitive-impaired adults. The tapes focus on long-term memory, with slow pacing and a visually uncluttered screen. Includes reminiscence, popular song, and simple hand and arm exercises. Available from: Innovative Caregiving Resources, P.O. Box 17332, Salt Lake City, UT 84117-0332; telephone 801-272-9446; range from $40.00 to $60.00 each.

ORGANIZATIONS

ABLEDATA

8455 Colesville Road, Suite 935
Silver Springs, MD 20910
800-227-0216
Direct TTY line 301-608-8912
301-608-8998
E-mail: belknap@macroint.com
URL: http://www.abledata.com

AbleData, a database of safe, accessible products, is funded by the federal government. Information on more than twenty thousand products is available by phone, mail, or on the Internet.

ALLIANCE FOR AGING RESEARCH

2021 K Street NW, Suite 305
Washington, DC 20006
202-293-2856

Call or write for free brochure "Incontinence, Everything You Wanted to Know but Were Afraid to Ask."

ALZHEIMER'S ASSOCIATION

919 North Michigan Avenue, Suite 1000
Chicago, IL 60611-1676
800-272-3900
E-mail: info@alz.org
URL: http://www.alz.org

Call for their catalog of tapes, booklets, books, brochures, and for the location of support groups and educational seminars in your area. In particular, the following free brochures are recommended:
ED207Z "Memory and Aging"
ED213Z "Caregiving at Home"
ED211Z "Alzheimer's Disease, an Overview"

ALZHEIMER'S DISEASE, EDUCATION AND REFERRAL CENTER (ADEAR)

P.O. Box 8250
Silver Springs, MD 20907-8250
800-438-4380
URL: http://www.alzheimers.org/adear

A division of the National Institute on Aging, ADEAR provides newsletters, brochures, and videos about the latest research findings on Alzheimer's disease and services for patients and their families. *Home Safety for the Alzheimer's Patient*, catalog no. A-11, is a 31-page brochure written in 1989 by the University of California in San Diego. It is available from ADEAR for $2.50, including shipping and handling.

AMERICAN ASSOCIATION OF RETIRED PERSONS (AARP)

601 E Street, NW
Washington, DC 20049
202-434-2277
800-424-3410
E-mail: aarpone@aol.com
URL: http://www.aarp.org

A national organization of members over fifty years of age, AARP sponsors volunteers under their Connections for Independent Living program to visit elders at home. AARP also produces many informative publications. The following is a partial listing of suggested materials:

Accessory Apartments (in press)
Connections Package: Don't Move, Improve! #D16237
A Consumer's Guide to Homesharing, #D12774
The DoAble Renewable Home, #D12470
Homemade Money: Consumer's Guide to Home Equity Conversion, #D12894
How to Protect Your Home, #D395
Selecting Retirement Housing, #D13680
Staying at Home: A Guide to Long-Term Care and Housing, #D14986

AMERICAN INSTITUTE OF ARCHITECTS (AIA)

1735 New York Avenue NW
Washington, DC 20006
202-626-7300
URL: http://www.aia.org

For help in finding an architect for home renovation.

AMERICAN SOCIETY OF INTERIOR DESIGNERS

608 Massachusetts Avenue NE
Washington, DC 20002-6006
800-610-2743
E-mail: network@asid.noli.com
URL: http://www.interiors.org

For help in locating an interior designer for barrier-free home modifications.

AMERICAN SOCIETY ON AGING

833 Market Street, Suite 511
San Francisco, CA 94103-1824
415-974-9600
URL: http://www.housecall.com/oac/asa

National organization dedicated to the rights and welfare of older adults. It sponsors yearly conferences around the country and publishes a quarterly journal entitled *Generations*.

AREA AGENCY ON AGING

800-677-1116

The U.S. Administration on Aging operates approximately 650 Area Agencies on Aging (AAA) throughout the country to help people locate services in their own communities. Many local AAA offices are listed under individual names, such as Department of Elder Affairs, Office on Aging, etc. For free information on services available to older people in your neighborhood, call the Eldercare Locator number listed above to find the office nearest you.

ARTHRITIS FOUNDATION

P.O. Box 19000
Atlanta, GA 30326
800-283-7800
URL: http://www.arthritis.org

Call or write for a listing of its free brochures.

ASTHMA AND ALLERGY FOUNDATION OF AMERICA

1125 Fifteenth Street NW, Suite 502
Washington, DC 20005
800-727-8462

Provides a bimonthly newsletter, pamphlets, and books.

Better Hearing Institute

5021 B Backlick Road
Annandale, VA 22003
800-943-2746

Call for free brochures, including "Your Guide to Better Hearing."

Center for Universal Design

North Carolina State University
P.O. Box 8613
Raleigh, NC 27695-8613
800-647-6777
E-mail: cahd@ncsu.edu
URL: http://www2.ncsu.edu/ncsu/design/cud

A national research, information, and training center, the Center for Universal Design has an extensive listing of brochures, newsletters, and other publications, including the "Housemate Agreement," TP#4.10, for $3.00, and a brochure on how to install grab bars, TP#1.10, $3.00.

Children of Aging Parents

Woodbourne Office Campus
1609 Woodbourne Road, Suite 302-A
Levittown, PA 19057-1511
800-227-7294

A national clearinghouse for information on caregiving issues for older adults, including referrals, support groups, and educational programs.

Christmas in April

1536 Sixteenth Street NW
Washington, DC 20036
800-473-4229

National program of volunteers assesses and modifies problems in the homes of low-income adults at no cost.

EASTERN PARALYZED VETERANS ASSOCIATION

75-20 Astoria Boulevard
Jackson Heights, NY 11270
718-803-3782

This organization provides design information on how to build a ramp for disabled veterans and nonveterans.

THE ELDERCARE LOCATOR

1112 Sixteenth Street NW, Suite 100
Washington, DC 20036
800-677-1116
Mon.–Fri. 9 A.M.–11 P.M. (Eastern Standard Time)

A trained information specialist refers callers to the appropriate state or local service, including Meals on Wheels, adult day care, senior center programs, housing choices, and home modification programs.

ELDERHOSTEL INSTITUTE NETWORK

Institute for Learning in Retirement (ILR)
56 Dover Road
Durham, NH 03824-3318
608-862-0725

A division of ElderHostel, the ILR fosters lifelong learning in local college campuses or in members' home. ILR offers a unique educational opportunity in which older adults define their own educational experiences; peer learning and teaching is an important foundation of the ILR philosophy. IRL encourages participation without regard to previous levels of education.

LIGHTHOUSE NATIONAL CENTER FOR VISION AND AGING

111 East Fifty-ninth Street
New York, NY 10022
212-821-9200
800-334-5497
E-mail: jjenkins@lighthouse.org
URL: http://www.lighthouse.org

The Lighthouse offers consultations on low-vision devices and rehabilitation classes on overcoming the effects of partial sight or blindness. Call for the nearest location in your community and for a free copy of the publications catalog. Their consumer mail-order catalog offers a wide choice of low-vision devices and household products.

National Association for Home Care

228 Seventh Street SE
Washington, DC 20003
202-547-7424
URL: http://www.nahc.org

Send a self-addressed stamped envelope for a free copy of "How to Choose a Home Care Agency: A Consumers' Guide."

National Association of Home Builders Research Center

400 Prince George's Boulevard
Upper Marlboro, MD 20772-8731
800-368-5242
URL: http://www.nahb.com

Provides an extensive list of publications and videos on new housing, remodeling, and accessible products. "Adaptable Fire-Safe House" VHS video of the center's adaptable, fire-safe house. $25.00, including an information packet.

National Association of Professional Geriatric Care Managers

1604 North Country Club Road
Tucson, AZ 85716-3102
520-881-8008

Geriatric care managers coordinate services to older adults; professional fees vary.

NATIONAL COUNCIL ON AGING

409 Third Street SW
Washington, DC 20024
202-479-1200
URL: http://www.ncoa.org

Organization dedicated to the well-being of older adults. Has extensive resources, including books and videos, for purchase on aging and housing issues.

NATIONAL HOSPICE ORGANIZATION

1901 North Moore Street, Suite 901
Arlington, VA 22209-1714
800-658-8898
URL: http://www.nho.org

Information about hospice care, including the location of the nearest agency in your neighborhood.

NATIONAL INSTITUTE ON AGING (NIA) INFORMATION CENTER

P.O. Box 8057
Gaithersburg, MD 20898-8057
800-222-2225
E-mail: niainfo@access.digex.net
URL: http://www.aoa.dhhs.gov/aoa.html

Disseminates free aging-related health information on numerous topics. A partial listing of their "Age Page" fact sheets:
"Aging and Your Eyes"
"Arthritis Advice"
"Forgetfulness in Old Age: It's Not What You Think"
"Hearing and Older People"
"Preventing Falls and Fractures"
"Stroke: Prevention and Treatment"

NATIONAL SHARED HOUSING RESOURCE CENTER

321 East Twenty-fifth Street
Baltimore, MD 21218
410-235-4454

For information about sharing your home with other people; produces several informational books, including *Shared Housing: A Planning Guide for Group Residences*. $25.00.

NATIONAL STROKE ASSOCIATION

96 Inverness Drive East, Suite I
Englewood, CO 80112-5112
800-787-6537
E-mail: info@stroke.org
URL: http://www.stroke.org

Produces informational brochures and a free guide, "Adaptive Resources: A Guide to Products and Services," for stroke survivors.

NURSING HOME INFORMATION SERVICE

National Senior Citizens Education and Research Center, Inc.
8403 Colesville Road
Silver Springs, MD 20910-3314
301-578-8800

An information and referral center for consumers of long-term care, their families, friends, and advocates. The service provides information on nursing homes and alternative community and health services, including a free guide on how to select a nursing home.

PROJECT LINK

Center for Assistive Technology
515 Kimball Tower
University at Buffalo
3435 Main Street
Buffalo, NY 14214-9980
800-628-2281

Free information service to help people learn about assistive products and where to get them. After filling out a questionnaire, Project Link will send you manufacturers' catalogs and brochures about helpful products related to your individual needs.

SENIORNET HEADQUARTERS

One Kearny Street, Third Floor
San Francisco, CA 94108
800-747-6848
415-352-1210
E-mail: seniornet@aol.com
URL: http://www.seniornet.org

A national nonprofit organization offering an on-line community for older adults. SeniorNet conducts computer training sessions for adults over fifty-five at eighty-five locations across the country and sponsors a yearly national conference.

INDEX

Page numbers in *italics* refer to illustration captions.

AARP, *see* American Association of Retired Persons

AbleData, 209

Ableware by Maddak, Inc., 178, 179, 181, 183, 184, 185, 186, 188, 193

Accessible Designs, 89, 183, 193

accessory apartments, 160, *160*

Access With Ease, 188, 190, 193

accidents, *see* safety and security

activity centers, 43–46
  for Alzheimer's patients, 136
  lighting in, 46–47

AdaptAbility, 178, 179, 180, 181, 182, 183, 185, 186, 187, 189, 193

age, in evaluating living space, 17

Aiphone Corp., 183, 193

air cleaners, 177

Alladin electronic magnifier, 133, *133*

allergies, 143–44
  bed covers for, 179

Alliance for Aging Research, 210

Altro Floors, 106, 182, 193

Alzheimer's Association, 210

Alzheimer's disease, 135–40

Alzheimer's Disease, Education and Referral Center (ADEAR), 210

American Association of Retired Persons (AARP), 24, 30, 153, 160, 162, 211
  Connections for Independent Living program of, 155

American Institute of Architects (AIA), 167, 211

American Society of Interior Designers, 165, 175, 211

American Society on Aging, 212

American Stair-Glide Corp., 37, 188, 189, 193

American Standard, 86, 100, 178, 179, 186, 191, 193

anticipation of future needs, in evaluating living space, 18

apartments, accessory, 160, *160*

appliances:
    electrical systems and, 33–34, 68
    kitchen, 82–88, 95
    see also specific appliances

Area Agencies on Aging (AAA), 150, 151, 155, 156, 212

Arjo-Century Inc., 178, 193

armoires and dressers, 45, 70

Armstrong World Inc., 182, 193

arthritis, 114

Arhtritis Foundation, 212

Asko, 85, 184, 194

A-Solution, Inc., 27, 193, 194

assisted living, 157, 173

Association of Home Appliance Manufacturers, 143–44

asthma, 143–44

Asthma and Allergy Foundation of America, 212

awnings, 189

BackSaver Products Co., 180, 191, 194

barrier-free home, 9
    checklist for evaluating, 13–14
    see also walker access; wheelchair access

bathroom, 9, 99–112
    elder, 108–10, *109*
    frailty and, 130–31
    grab bars in, 102, 108, 111, *112*, 121, *121*, 178
    mental impairment and, 138–39
    mobility limitations and, 118, 121
    modular, *109*, 110, 178
    new, planning of, 101–6
    products for, 110–12
    renovating of, 106–8
    resource guide to products for, 178–79
    showers in, *see* showers
    sinks in, 102–3, 179
    toilets in, *see* toilets
    tubs in, *see* bathtubs

visual limitations and, 134
wheelchair users and, 125

Bathroom Access, 178, 179, 194

bathtubs, 104, 178
    chairs for, 110, 111, *111*, 178, 179
    grab bars for, 108, 111, *112*, 178
    lifts for, 111, 178

bats, 62, 189

bedroom, 65–76, 66
    dressing in, 69–70, 118, 179
    exercising in, 70–73, 181
    frailty and, 131
    as healing place, 75–76
    hearing limitations and, 141
    leisure time in, 67–69
    mental impairment and, 139–40
    mobility limitations and, 118, 122
    resource guide to products for, 179–80
    sleeping in, 73–75
    visual limitations and, 134
    wheelchair users and, 125

beds, 73–75
    electric, 74, 139, 147
    handrails for, 73, 179
    height of, 74, 179
    lamp near, 73–74
    mattresses for, 74–75, 179, 180
    pillows for, 68, 74, 179, 180
    rising from, 73
    tables and, 73–74, 147, 180
    views from, 68–69

berms, 62

Besam, Inc., 180, 194

Better Hearing Institute, 213

bidets, 178

birds, 62

B. J. Industries, Inc., 186, 194

Block Nurse Program, 156

board and care homes, 157

Broan Manufacturing Inc., 105, 178, 194

Brookstone, 181, 182, 187, 188, 190, 193, 194

Bruce Medical Supply, 192, 194

Bruno Independent Living Aids, 189, 194

budget, 18–19
    twenty-thousand-dollar, 21
    two-thousand-dollar, 20

bugs, 62–63

butterflies, 62
buying or renting a new home, 163–64, 172–76

Cabinetmate, 91
cabinets, kitchen, 88, 89, *89*, 90–92, 116, 183
    countertops, 80, 88–90, *89*, 183
Cambridge Brass, 184, 194
canes, 126, *126*, 188
    holders for, 188
Carmel Homes, 161, 182, 194
carpeting, 38, 42, 72, 181
    patterns in, 136
    shag, 72
carton holders, 185
carts, 183
cataracts, 132
Center for Universal Design, 213
Cervitor Kitchens Inc., 185, 194
chair lifts, 119, *120*, 188
chairs, 41, 67, 191
    in bathroom, 108, 112
    bathtub/shower, 110, 111, *111*, 178, 179
    reclining, 41, 46, 191
    rising devices for, 41, 67, 191
    rocking, 136, *136*, 191
Chef's Catalog, 186, 187, 194
Chicago Faucet Co., 137, 184, 195
Children of Aging Parents, 213
Christmas in April, 151, 213
circuit breakers and service panels, 34, 95
Clarion Fiberglass, 179, 195
cleaning utensils, 182
Clensicair, 142, *142*, 182
closet hangers, 125, *125*, 179
closets, 45, 69–70, 118
    organizers for, 69, 179, 187
clothes, velcro, 179
Coastal Colony Corporation, 161, 182, 195
coefficient of friction (COF), 38, 94, 105–6
coffee makers, 183
coffee tables, 42
co-housing, 157
    information sources on, 158
Collins & Alkman, 181, 195
color, 11, 41
    contrasting, checklist for evaluating, 16

light and, 47
    as safety factor, 11, 16, 42, 43
communes, senior, 157
communication systems, 28–30
    emergency response, 29–30, 105, 181
    intercoms, 26, 30, 183
    telephones, *see* telephones
community, 149–62
    companionship in, 154–55
    finding resources in, 150–56
    grocery and meal preparation services in, 152
    health care and life-management services in, 155–56
    home repair and maintenance programs in, 151–52
    house sharing in, 156–61
    recreation and leisure in, 153–54
    transportation services in, 152–53
companionship, 154–55
computer centers, 43–45, *44*
Consumer's Guide to High-Tech Home Health Care, A, 144
containers, 183
Container Store, 179, 187, 195
continuing care retirement communities (CCRCs), 173
cookbooks, 184
cooktops, *see* stoves and cooktops
countertops, 80, 88–90, *89*, 183
Crest Electronics, Inc., 72–73, 178, 180, 187, 188, 189, 191, 195
crime prevention, 24
cups, 184
cutting boards, 96, 97, 184

day care centers, 154
deck lighting, 190
decks, 54
Delta Faucet Co., 184, 195
dementia, 135–40
desk lamps, 187
desk space, 46
diabetes, 132
dishes, 117, *117*, 120–21, 183, 186
    cups and mugs, 184, 185
    utensils, 185, 187
dishwashers, 85, 184

doorbells, 27, 180
  for hearing impaired, 27, 140, *141*, 180
doorknobs and doorhandles, 115, *115*, 180
doors, 37
  automatic openers for, 180–81
  bathroom, 101
  exterior, 24–25
  hinges for, 181
  locks for, 26, 181
  pockets, 37, 101
  resource guide to products for, 180–81
  screen, 25
  sliding, 25
doorways, 37, 119, *120*
  wheelchair access and, 24, 37
Walter Drake & Sons, 181, 187, 190, 195
drapery opening units, 193
drawer pulls and handles, 70, 116
dressers and armoires, 45, 70
dressing, 69–70, 118
  aids for, 179
  see also closets
Dristar, 142, *142*, 183
Drive 55, 153
dryers and washers, 88, 105, 187
Durasol Systems, Inc., 189, 195
Dwyer Products, 185, 195

Eastern Paralyzed Veterans Association, 52,
    214
eating aids, 117, *117*, 120–21, 183, 184–
    185, 186
ECHO (Elder Cottage Housing Opportunity),
    160–61, 182
Econol Stairway Lift Corp., 188, 189, 195
The Eden Alternative, 162
The Eldercare Locator, 151, 156, 175, 214
elder cottages, 160–61
ElderHostel Institute Network, 154, 214
electrical cords, 42
  extension, 34, 42, 45, 68, 95
electrical systems, 33–34
  in bathroom, 105
  home hospital equipment and, 147
  in kitchen, 95
  outlets in, 34, 45, 68, 95
Electric Mobility, 189, 195
elevators, 37, 189

Elkay Products, 86, 186, 195
emergency response systems, 29–30, 105,
    181
emphysema, 143–44
Enrichments, 97, 178, 179, 180, 183, 184,
    185, 186, 187, 188, 191, 195
environmental controls, 30–35, 181
  see also electrical systems; light, lighting;
    temperature
equity conversion mortgages, 169–70
exercise, 70–73, 128
  equipment for, 72, 181
extension cords, 34, 42, 45, 68, 95
exterior protection, 24–28
eyesight, *see* visual limitations

fabric patterns, 136
falls, 10, 29, 35, 128
fans, bathroom, 105, 178
faucets, 103, 104, 107–8, 137, 184
  sensor-activated, 108, 184
  turners for, 117, *117*, 184
Fellowship for Intentional Community, 158
Fiatarone, Maria, 71
fire extinguishers, 93
fire safety, 10
  halogen floor lamps and, 32
  in kitchen, 92–93
  smoke alarms and, 35, 92, 192
  smoking and, 41, 93
fire suppressant systems, 93, 185
Fitz Hang, 125, *125*, 179, 196
Flinchbaugh Company, Inc., 189, 196
floodlights, 190
floors, flooring, 38, 182
  in bathroom, 105–6
  in bedroom, 71
  carpeting, *see* carpeting
  friction ratings of, 38, 94, 105–6
  in kitchen, 94
  resource guide for, 181–82
  rugs on, 38, 42, 72
  safety and, 38, 94
  wood, 38, 94
flower boxes, 190
foam handles, tubular, 118, *118*, 185
food preparation, 116–17, 119–20
  community programs and, 152

Forbo Industries, 182, 196
forks, 185
frailty, 128–31
freezers, 85, 116
friendship centers, 153–54
Frigidaire Co., 184, 186, 187, 196
furniture:
    chairs, *see* chairs
    coffee tables, 42
    for living areas, 41–43
    outdoor, 61
    sofas, 46, 191
fuses, fuse boxes, 33, 34, 95

games, 45
    resource guide for, 182
garage, 28, 53
garage door openers, 28
garbage and trash disposal, 84–85, 185
Gardener's Supply Co., 187, 189, 190, 196
gardens, gardening, 56–62
    container, 59–60, 190
    pathways and walkways in, *25*, 53, 136
    tools for, 58, *58*, 190
    vertical, hanging, and tabletop, 60
gas heating systems, 34
GE Appliances, 184, 185, 186, 187, 196
geriatric care managers, 155–56
glare, 10, 33, 46, 47, 68, 95
glaucoma, 131–32
grab bars, 9
    in bathroom, 102, 108, 111, *112*, 121,
        121, 178
    folding, 178
    wall hung, 178
    see also handrails
Graeff, Robert, 109–10, 178, 196
graters, 185
Great Lakes Plastic, 107, 179, 196
Grohe America, Inc., 184, 196
Guardian, 189, 196

halogen lights, 32
    safety tips for, 32
Hammacher Schlemmer, 183, 186, 187, 196
Hanchett Entry Systems, 26, 181, 196
handles, foam rubber, 118, *118*, 185
handrails (railings), 9–10, 189

for beds, 73, 179
for long walls, 72–73
for stairs and steps, *25*, 50
    see also grab bars
hangers, extended, 125, *125*, 179
Hare, Patrick, 159
healing, bedroom as place for, 75–76,
    145–47, *146*
health care services, 155–56
health conditions, 113–48
    allergies, asthma, and emphysema, 143–
        144, 179
    in evaluating living space, 17–18
    general frailty, 128–31
    hearing limitations, *see* hearing limitations
    home care and, 144–47, *146*
    home hospice and, 147–48
    incontinence, 142–43, 182–83
    memory and thinking impairment, 135–40
    mobility limitations, *see* mobility
        limitations
    visual limitations, *see* visual limitations
hearing limitations, 140–41
    doorbells for, 27, 140, *141*, 180
heating systems, 31
    gas, 34
    radiant panels, 31, 182
    resource guide for, 182
heat lamps, 105
Hebrew Rehabilitation Center, 71
Hill Rom, *142*, 182, 196
Hitec Group International, Inc., 180, 196
hobbies and interests, 43–45
    resource guide for, 182
holders, carton, 185
Home Automation Systems Inc., 183, 188,
    190, 192, 193, 197
HomeCare suites, 161, 182
Homecrest Healthcare, 127, *127*, 189, 197
The Home Depot, 45
home equity loans, 169–70
home modification:
    community programs for repair, mainte-
        nance and, 151–52
    see also renovation and modification
Home Trends, 182, 183, 186, 187, 188, 193,
    197
Honeywell, Inc., 177, 181, 183, 187, 197

hospice, home, 147–48
hospital room, home, 144–47, *146*
hot-water dispensers, 87
house members, in evaluating living space, 18
house sharing, 156–61
    information sources on, 159
    physical space remedies for, 159–61
housing units, 182
    ECHO, 160–61, 182
    HomeCare suites, 161, 182
Ted Hoyer & Co., Inc., 189, 197

IKEA, 45, 185, 197
ILA: Independent Living Aids, 178, 179,
    180, 181, 182, 184, 185, 186, 187,
    188, 189, 190, 191, 192, 197
incontinence, 142–43
    resource guide to products for, 182–83
insects, 62–63
In-Step Mobility Products, Inc., 197
Institutes for Learning in Retirement (ILR),
    154
intercom systems, 26, 30
    resource guide for, 183
Interim Healthcare, 181, 197
Intermed Allstate, 183, 197
Ironmonger, 181, 197

jar openers, 185
Jay Care, 127, 189
Jay Medical Ltd., 127, 189, 197
Jenn-Air, 85, 184, 187, 197
Joint Adventure, 180, 197

Kenmore, 184, 185
key chains and holders, 181
Kindred Ind., 86, 186, 198
kitchen, 77–97, *78*, *130*
    appliances in, 82–88, 95
    cabinets in, 88, 89, *89*, 90–92, 116, 183
    frailty and, 129–30
    gadgets and ideas for, 96–97
    hearing limitations and, 141
    layout and design of, 79–82, 89
    mental impairment and, 137–38
    mobility limitations and, 116–17, 119–21
    ovens in, *see* ovens
    resource guide to products for, 183–87
    safety in, 81–82, 92–95, 137
    sinks in, 86–87, 186
    stoves and cooktops in, *see* stoves and
        cooktops
    units, 87, *160*, 185
    visual limtations and, 133–34
    wheelchair users and, 124
    work surfaces (countertops) in, 80, 88–90,
        89, 183
KitchenAid, 84, 184, 185, 198
Kmart, 188
knives, 96, 97, 185
Kohler Co., 178, 184, 198
KraftMaid, 183, 198
Kwikset, 181

lamps, 42, 47, 68
    bedside, 73–74
    extra wall switches for, 34, *34*
    floor (torchères), 32, 47, 67
    touch-turn-on devices for, 47, 67, 68,
        188
    see also light, lighting
laundry facilities, 105
lavender oil, 180
leg-lifter straps, 189
leisure time:
    bedroom as place for, 67–69
    community programs and, 153–54
Lifeline, 181, 198
life-management services, 155–56
lifts, 119, *120*, 122, 188, 189
light, lighting, 10, 30–33, 46–47
    in bathroom, 105, 108
    in bedroom, 67, 68
    checklist for evaluating, 15
    in closet, 69
    in computer center, 44, *44*
    fluorescent, 32, 90
    glare and, 10, 33, 46, 47, 68, 95
    halogen, 32
    in kitchen, 90, 94–95
    in living areas, 46–47
    outdoor, *25*, 27–28, 53, 190
    quality of, 10
    resource guide for, 187–88
    sensor, 33, 47, 188
    on stairs, 36, 51

wall switches for, 34, *34*, 74, 95, 115, *115*, 188
  see also lamps
Lighthouse Consumer Products Catalogue, 97, 182, 183, 184, 185, 186, 187, 191, 192, 198
Lighthouse National Center for Vision and Aging, 132, 214–15
Lillian Vernon, 181, 186, 198
Linido USA, 178, 198
living areas, 39–43, *40*
  frailty and, 129
  furniture in, 41–43
  hearing limitations and, 140–41
  lighting in, 46–47; see also light, lighting
  mental impairment and, 135–37
  mobility limitations and, 115–16, 119
  visual limitations and, 132–33
  wheelchair users and, 123–24
Living at Home/Block Nurse Program, 156
locks, 26, 181
Logan Powell Co., 186, 198
Lubidet, *139*

macular degeneration, 131–32
magnifiers, 133, *133*, 191
Malber U.S.A., Inc., 187, 198
manufacturers and suppliers, list of, 193–202
mattresses, 74–75, 180
  pads and covers for, 179, 180
Maxi-Aids, 178, 179, 180, 181, 182, 183, 184, 185, 186, 187, 188, 191, 192, 198
Maytag/Admiral Products, 184, 187, 198
  Jenn-Air, 85, 184, 187, 197
meal preparation, 116–17, 119–20
  community programs and, 152
Meals on Wheels, 152
Medchair, 142
medicine cabinets, 111
mental impairment, 135–40
Metropolitan Center for Independent Living, 53
microwave ovens, 83–84, 95, 185
minimal effort test, 10–11, 15–16
minivan services, 153
Minivator, 37
mirrors, 112
Mobile Care, Inc., 161, 182, 191, 198

mobility limitations, 35–38, 114–27
  minimal effort test and, 10–11, 15–16
  minor, 115–18
  resource guide to products for, 188–89
  serious, 118–22
  specialized aids for, 125–27
  see also wheelchair access
modification, home:
  community programs for repair, maintenance and, 151–52
  see also renovation and modification
Moen Inc., 178, 198
mortgage, reverse, 169–70
moving to a new home, 163–64, 172–76
mugs, 185
R. C. Musson Rubber Co., 182, 199
mylar film, 33, 193

naps, 46
National Association for Home Care (NAHC), 144–45, 215
National Association of Area Agencies on Aging, 150
National Association of Home Builders (NAHB), 167, 215
National Association of Professional Geriatric Care Managers, 156, 175, 215
National Council on Aging, 216
National Directory of Home Modification and Repair Programs, The, 152
National Fiber Glass Products, 179, 184, 199
National Hospice Organization, 216
National Institute on Aging (NIA), 162, 216
National Resource and Policy Center on Housing and Long-Term Care, 152
National Shared Housing Resource Center, 157, 159, 217
National Stroke Association, 217
National Wheel-O-Vator Co., 189, 199
night-lights, 74, 188
Nor-Am Patient Care Products Ltd., 189, 199
North Coast Medical, Inc., 178, 179, 183, 184, 185, 186, 187, 189, 190, 199
NT Dor-O-Matic, Inc., 180, 199
Nursing Home Information Service, 162, 217
nursing homes, 161–62
  information sources on, 162

Nursing Home Without Walls, 156
Nutone, 180, 199

oil, lavender, 180
outdoor spaces, 49–63
    checklist for evaluating, 12–13
    frailty and, 129
    furniture in, 61
    gardens, *see* gardens, gardening
    lighting for, 25, 27–28, 53, 190
    mobility limitations and, 119
    pathways and walkways in, 25, 53,
        136
    porches, 25, 56, 63, 190
    resource guide to products for, 189–90
    transition from indoors to, 50–56
    visual limitations and, 132
    wheelchair users and, 123–24
ovens, 82–83, 187
    knob turners for, 117, *117*, 185
    microwave, 83–84, 95, 185
    see also stoves and cooktops

page-turning device, 119, 191
pans and pots, 97, *97*, 186
Parkinson's disease, 114, 126
Pathfinder Enterprises, Inc., 127, 189,
    199
pathways and walkways, 25, 53
    mental impairment and, 136
patios, 54–56
patterns in fabric and carpeting, 136
peelers, 186
Perfectly Safe, 179, 188, 191, 199
Performa Home, 181, 199
physical condition, *see* health conditions
physical support, *see* support
pill alarms, 191
pillows, 68, 74, 180
    covers for, 179
planter boxes, 59–60, 190
Planter Technology, 190, 199
porches, 25, 56, 63, 190
pots and pans, 97, *97*, 186
Pressalit System, *100*, 103, 179
Primarily Seating, 191, 199
product resource list, 177–93
Project Link, 217–18

railings, *see* handrails
Raisin' Cane, Inc., 126, *126*, 188, 199
ramps, *51*, 52–53, 189, 190
RCA Rubber Co., 182, 199
reachers, long-handled, 96, 116, *116*, 186
reading aids, 46, 68
    magnifiers, 133, *133*, 191
    page-turning device, 119, 191
    resource guide for, 191
reading in bed, pillows for, 68, 180
Reaffirming Citizen Power, 156
receptacles, 191
recreational programs, 153–54
refrigerators, 85, 95, 116, 186
Rehab Seating Systems, Inc., 191, 200
Reliable Home Office, 45, 183, 187, 200
remote control units, 188
renovation and modification, 163, 164–65,
    166–71
    budget for, 18–19
    community assistance programs for, 151–
        152
    financing of, 169–70
    tips for surviving construction in, 171
    twenty-thousand-dollar budget for, 21
    two-thousand-dollar budget for, 20
renting or buying a new home, 163–64,
    172–76
resources, 177–202
    community, finding of, 150–56
    manufacturers and suppliers, 193–202
    product list, 177–93
retirement communities, 173
Rock 'N' Go, 127, *127*, 189
Rohl Corporation, 184, 200
roommates, 158–59
room temperature, *see* temperature
rugs, 38, 42, 72
rummaging, 136

safety and security, 23–38
    in bathroom, 100
    checklist for evaluating, 14
    communication systems, *see* communication
        systems
    environmental controls, 30–35, 181; *see*
        also electrical systems; light, lighting;
        temperature

exterior production, 24–28
falls and, 10, 29, 35, 128
fires and, *see* fire safety
flooring and, 38, 94
halogen floor lamps and, 32
in kitchen, 81–82, 92–95, 137
mental impairment and, 136–37
mobility and, *see* mobility
physical support and, 9–10
Sammons Preston, 184, 185, 187, 200
Sauder Manufacturing Company, *136*, 191,
 200
Schlage Lock Co., 181, 200
scooters, powered, 127, 189
Screen Tight, 63, 190, 200
Sears Home Health Care, 177, 178, 179,
 180, 181, 186, 189, 191, 192, 200
Sears Home Improvement and Appliances,
 183, 185, 186, 187, 188, 189, 190,
 192, 200
seating:
 chairs, *see* chairs
 resource guide for, 191
 sofas, 46, 191
security, *see* safety and security
Select Comfort, 180, 200
Self Care Catalog, 179, 182, 200
SeniorNet Headquarters, 218
Senior Style, 191, 200
sensor lighting, 33, 47, 188
service panels and circuit breakers, 34, 95
shared housing, *see* house sharing
Sharp Electronics Corp., 200
Sharper Image, 181, 185, 187, 200
showers, 104–5, *104*, 107–8, 179
 antiscald controls for, 107, 137, 179
 chairs for, 110, 111, *111*, 178, 179
 handheld units, 107, 111, 178
sinks:
 bathroom, 102–3, 179
 faucets of, 103, 108, 117, *117*, 137, 184
 kitchen, 86–87, 186
sleeping, 73–75
 naps, 46
Smith & Nephew Rehabilitation, 178, 179,
 180, 182, 184, 186, 187, 189, 201
smoke alarms, 35, 92, 192
smoking, 41, 93

soap dispensers, 112, 179
sofas, 46, 191
space heaters, 31, 34
Speakman, 184, 201
SSHC, Inc., 182, 201
stairs and steps, 35–37, *36*, 50–52
 handrails for, *25*, 50
 lighting on, 36, 51
 mental impairment and, 135
 treads for, 35, 182
stools, 96, *96*, 186
storage, 45, 68
 bathroom, 111–12
 closet, 45, 69–70
 kitchen cabinets, 88, 89, *89*, 90–92, 116,
 183
stoves and cooktops, 82–83, 93, 137, 184
 fire suppressant systems for, 93, 185
 see also ovens
strength training, 71
suppliers and manufacturers, list of, 193–202
support, 9–10
 checklist for evaluating, 14
 see also grab bars; handrails

tablecloths, 190
tables:
 bedside, 73–74
 fold-up, 186
 mobile, 147, 180
Tarkett, Inc., 182, 201
Tavac Manufacturing, 183, 201
tea kettles, 186, 187
Techni-Floe, Inc., 142, 183, 201
Tele Larm, Inc., 191, 201
telephones, 29, 43
 in bathroom, 105, 108
 bedside, 68
 emergency assistance units for, 29–30, 181
 mental impairment and, 136
 resource guide for telephone accessories
 and, 192
telephone services, 155
television, 45–46, 133
 resource guide to products for, 192
temperature, 30, 31, 43
 heating systems and, 31, 34
Tempur-Pedic, 180, 201

Thermador, 184, 185, 201
thermostats, 182
thinking impairment, 135–40
Thomasville Furniture, 191, 201
timers, 186, 190
toaster ovens, 187
toilets, 103
    bidets for, 178
    cleansing attachments for, 139, *139*
    grab bars for, 102, 108, 121, *121*, 178
torchères (floor lamps), 47, 67
    halogen, 32
The Toro Company, 190, 201
Toto Kiki Usa, Inc., 178, 201
Touch Turner, 119, 191, 201
touch-turn-on devices, 47, 67, *68*, 188
towels, 112
transportation services, 152–53
trash and garbage disposal, 84–85, 185
trellis/teepee kits, 60, 190
Trex Co., 54, 190, 201
Tru-Value, 188
Twenty-first Century, 185, 202

U-Step Walker Stabilizer, 126
utensils, 185, 187

vanities, 111
velcro clothes, 179
ventilation, bathroom, 105
    fans, 105, 178
Lillian Vernon, 181, 186, 198
visiting services, 155
visual limitations, 131–34
    color and, 11; *see also* color
    lighting and, 10; *see also* light, lighting

Waldmann Lighting, 187, 202
walker access, 9, 37
    toilet and, 102, 103
walkers, 126, 189
walkways and pathways, *25*, 53
    mental impairment and, 136
Wal-Mart, 188
Walter Drake & Sons, 181, 187, 190, 195
Warm Rain, 107
washers and dryers, 88, 105, 187
watering systems, 58, 190
water temperature:
    antiscald controls and, 107, 137, 179
    hot-water dispensers and, 87
WayMaker, 127
Weiser Lock, 181, 202
Welbilt Appliance Corp., 184, 187, 202
Wenzelite Medical Supply Corp., 189, 202
wheelchair access, 9, 115, 123–25
    bed height and, 74
    doorways and, 24, 37
    toilet and, 103
wheelchairs, 114, 126–27, *127*, 189
Whirlpool Corp., 184, 186, 202
    KitchenAid, 84, 184, 185, 198
Whitaker Co., 178, 180, 188, 189, 191, 202
White Home Products, Inc., 179, 202
windows, 26–27, 43
    resource guide to products for, 193
    see also light, lighting
Windsor Feeder, 121
wiring, *see* electrical systems

Yorktowne Cabinets, 183, 202